A GUIDEBOOK TO THE
NORTHERN CALIFORNIA COAST

*Volume II, Humboldt and
Del Norte Counties*

*Pebble Beach is a photographer's delight.
Typically, on a summer evening the sun emerges
briefly from behind a curtain of coastal fog
before it sinks into the sea.*

A GUIDEBOOK *to the*

NORTHERN CALIFORNIA

COAST

VOLUME II

Humboldt and Del Norte Counties

BY MIKE HAYDEN

Edited and with a preface by RUSS LEADABRAND

THE WARD RITCHIE PRESS · LOS ANGELES

THIS BOOK IS

DEDICATED TO

MARY

COPYRIGHT © 1970 BY MIKE HAYDEN
Library of Congress Catalog Card Number 77-125196
International Standard Book Number 378-03052-3
Printed in the United States of America

CONTENTS

PREFACE

A GUIDEBOOK TO THE NORTHERN CALIFORNIA COAST • VOLUME II

by Mike Hayden

In two pocket-sized volumes, this guide explores the coast of Northern California from Muir Beach near San Francisco's Golden Gate to Pelican Beach on the border with Oregon.

The first volume of the guide follows California Highway 1 up the coast of Marin, Sonoma, and Mendocino Counties. Volume II deals mainly with the Humboldt-Del Norte Coast where much of the seashore is remote from the main routes of travel.

Volume I ends and this book begins at Rockport, an old lumber center on the Mendocino Coast, 27 miles north of Fort Bragg. The break occurs at Rockport because this is where California 1 swings away from the ocean to join the US 101 Redwood Highway at Leggett.

This guide concentrates mainly on the oceanside and outer Coast Ranges. So instead of following Highway 1 to Leggett, we leave the asphalt a few miles beyond Rockport and switch to low gear on the steep unpaved Usal Road. This ridge route follows the coastline to a rural junction near the Mendocino-Humboldt County line.

Some stretches of the Humboldt-Del Norte Coast are roadless. Where these occur, the book lists foot trails which approach the seashore. As in Volume I, the possibilities for camping, hunting, fishing, boating, and beachcombing are listed, together with advice on where stores, restaurants, and commercial accommodations may be found.

Part V

Most of this 55-mile coast is roadless, but there are places where the road-bound explorer may sample the seashore. Hunting, fishing, and hiking are the main attractions. ¶ There are several roadside camps in the King Range, a trailer park and modern motel at Shelter Cove, and some rustic accommodations in the Mattole River Country.

CHAPTER 15: USAL   Two miles up the Shoreline Highway from Rockport is a demonstration forest of the Redwood Council. It has a picnic area and self-guiding nature trail. A bit farther, the pavement spans the North Fork of Cottoneva Creek.

A short piece across the bridge on the lefthand side of the road, a dim, narrow forest lane that is neither signed nor paved climbs steeply into the woods. This is Usal Road. It substitutes for the Shoreline Highway on the northern twenty miles of the Mendocino Coast.

The Usal Road isn't shown on most oil company maps. But it was a vital link in the sketchy road system which joined Eureka with the San Francisco Bay Area before the Redwood Highway was completed in the 1920's.

A proper road system was slow to develop on the North Coast, partly because the lumber kings found it more convenient to ship by schooner. The sheep ranchers were fearful that roads would encourage settlement and force a rise in taxes.

Near the county line, the Usal Road connects with other byways which permit the traveler to approach Eureka by way of the King Range, Mattole River, and lonely Cape Mendocino.

The Usal Road hasn't changed much since Jack London and

9

his wife, Charmian, drove it in a horse-drawn carriage on a trip to Eureka in 1911. It has some fierce grades and many twists and turns, but the surface isn't half bad after the county works on it in Spring. The drive isn't recommended for low-slung sports cars and hauling a trailer is out of the question. There are no towns, stores, or any settlement to speak of before you cross the county line.

An easier approach to the King Range and the Mattole River country is by way of the Shelter Cove Road which leaves the Redwood Highway near Garberville. This road is being developed as an all-weather route and is suitable for trailers.

The gas stop nearest the Usal Road on Highway 1 is four miles east of the turn-off at Hales Grove. A small store and resort is located near the intersection with a high-speed logging road of the Union Lumber Company. The truck drivers who patronize the short order restaurant here are apt to be informed about conditions on the Usal Road.

Logging trucks may be encountered on the Usal Road but they won't run as large as those which travel the private road. These monster diesels carry up to 120,000 pounds of logs, which is far above the legal limit permitted on public thoroughfares.

From Highway 1, the Usal Road climbs with a minimum of switchbacks to a ridgetop that crests 1,000 feet above the sea. Here there's a break in the forest where sheep and cattle graze. This clearing and other openings along the route afford some spectacular views of the coast when it isn't fogging. In Spring, the roadsides are edged with foxgloves, columbines, and yellow monkey flowers. Ferns and blackberry brambles are thick in places.

On the five-mile drive to Usal, the road contours along the ridgetop, passing through young stands of Douglas fir that are signed, "POISON AND BEAR TRAPS."

*Steep meadows off the Usal Road plunge
precipitously to the sea. The flowers are foxgloves.*

For centuries, the forest primeval withstood the depredations of chipmunks, squirrels, porcupines, deer, and "Smokey the Bear," without any help from man. But the modern forester deems it necessary to wage war on these creatures to obtain the maximum timber yield.

In a series of abrupt turns, the road drops to the meadows at Usal Creek where some decaying sheds and a horse barn are the only vestiges of settlement. The frontage is private and access for rockfishing and smelt netting may be revoked at any time.

J. H. Wonderly built a redwood mill at Usal in 1889, together with a 1600-foot wharf and three miles of logging railway. The mill and property were purchased by Captain Robert Dollar in 1894.

Usal was one of the most treacherous of the "doghole ports." The reluctance of shipping companies to permit their vessels to call here prompted Captain Dollar to acquire his own fleet. Dollar's first ship was the 218-ton steam schooner, Newsboy, built to his order at San Francisco in 1888. The talented skipper who took command was Captain "Hoodlum" Bob Walvig, so-called because he was quick to denounce any crewman who questioned his orders as a "hoodlum."

The first steam schooners were conventional schooners with an engine and boiler added as an afterthought. Auxiliary power gave these little ships a maneuverability without which it would have been impossible to navigate the more difficult ports.

Steam schooners were first used on the North Coast in 1864. By 1880, they dominated the coastwise trade. Few of these vessels exceeded 1,000 tons.

Two well-preserved veterans of the lumber trade are permanently docked at San Francisco's Maritime State Historical Park, located at the foot of Hyde Street near Fisherman's Wharf. These

12

are the steam schooner Wapama and the C. A. Thayer, a conventional three-masted schooner.

Presently, the coastwise lumber trade supports only two self-propelled barges, operated by the O. J. Olson Company of San Mateo.

Shortly after the Usal Mill closed in 1902, it was destroyed by fire. Most of the town burned with it. The schooner Newsboy sank in 1906 as the result of a collision with the Wasp on Humboldt Bay. By then, Captain Dollar had acquired the steam schooner, Grace Dollar, forerunner of the Dollar Line's globe-circling fleet of sixty freighters and passenger liners. In 1938, this fleet was taken over by the American President Lines.

According to Kroeber, the name Usal is a Pomo word meaning "south." It was the name used by the settlers for the Sinkyone Indians who had a village at Usal.

From Usal, the road runs four miles up Timber Ridge, climbing to 1,555 feet before it drops to a small bench above Mistake Point. Here a rugged spur angles down the side of Anderson Cliff to a mill site on Jackass Creek. Access for fishing and smelt netting is by permission of the land owner.

From the bench, it's a long, slow eleven miles to Four Corners by way of Jackass Ridge. The road ascends to a high of 1,864 feet on the ridge but touches few points where the timber allows a view of the coast. A topographical map comes in handy on this leg of the drive because of the numerous logging spurs. Some may easily be confused with the main road.

There's nothing at Four Corners except a junction. The Usal Road ends here. The Chamise Mountain Road, which is signed Route 431, continues north, crossing the Humboldt-Mendocino County line two miles north of the junction. This road passes several public campgrounds on the east slope of the King Range before it joins the Shelter Cove Road.

The road to the left of the junction is closed by a private gate. It angles south, losing 1,370 feet in elevation on a 5½-mile descent to Bear Harbor. Calvin Stewart, the pioneer lumberman who helped C. R. Johnson get started at Fort Bragg, settled here in 1893. Presently, there's a ranch at Bear Harbor and, at last report, the owners were planning to develop a resort. The black sand beach at Bear Harbor is completely inundated at high tide.

On the right of the junction is the Briceland Road which is signed Route 435. It's a five-mile drive on this unpaved road to the general store at Thorn. A sleepy hamlet, Thorn is situated on the upper Mattole River where it first rises in the Whitethorn Valley.

CHAPTER 16: THE KING RANGE From the vicinity of Four Corners, the mountains of the King Range stretch 25 miles up the coast, almost to the mouth of the Mattole River.

These mountains are exceptionally rugged. Their foggy, wind-blown Pacific slopes rise directly from the ocean at angles of 45 degrees or steeper. No improved roads challenge these grades except the Shelter Cove Road which snakes down to the isolated marine terrace at Point Delgada. The highest mountain is Kings Peak. It crests at 4,086 feet.

Roughly two-thirds of the King Range, numbering 31,500 acres, is federal land administered by the Bureau of Land Management. The summit and west slope is maintained as wilderness. Sheep grazing is permitted but the only improvements are trails and campsites.

Some of the longer trails invite backpacking. The primitive camps scattered along the summit are most heavily used during the deer season. The King Range abounds with blacktail deer but it's not easy country to hunt. A horse or mule is needed to pack out the kill. When the season opens in August, the legal bucks are apt to be concentrated in high places. The BLM recommends Chamise Mountain, Queens Peak, and Kings Peak.

The densely forested east slope is managed for recreation and timber cutting. All the streams here are tributary to the Mattole River.

Spreading north and east of the King Range is a rough hinterland which is penetrated by few roads other than jeep trails and logging spurs.

The resident Indians on the coast were the Sinkyone tribe of the Athabascans. They were ruthlessly hunted down by the early settlers and federal troops until virtually exterminated. The practice was to kill the men and send the women and children to remote reservations.

15

Chamise Mountain Trail runs five miles from
Wailaki Campground to an isolated beach at the
mouth of Chamise Creek.

On February 20, 1864, the Humboldt Times at Eureka reported that, "Lt. Frazier, Co. E, C.M., with a detachment of twelve men stationed at Upper Mattole, started on a scout about the 1st. instant, and the night of the second succeeded in finding some Indians at Whitethorn Valley, on the Mattole River about 25 miles south of Upper Mattole. At this place, he captured thirteen squaws and killed four bucks—none escaping. The Indians offered no resistance, being completely surprised."

Among the older generation on the North Coast, many will defend the policy of genocide. A harsh assessment of the Coast tribes is found in the regional history, "Lure of the Humboldt Bay Region," by Chad L. Hoopes of Loleta. According to Hoopes, "Those Indians living along the Coast were an inferior civilization; they were thriftless, idle, and debased, usually provoking the unmerciful vengeance of the settlers by petty thievery."

Alfred Kroeber in his "Handbook of the Indians of California" allows the Sinkyone were "backwoodsmen," culturally less advanced than the Pomos. But he suggests this was so because they lived a marginal existence in country less bountiful than the Pomo territory.

The Sinkyone built their villages on the best land available, such as the meadow at Usal and the terrace at Shelter Cove. They resorted to stealing only after the settlers pre-empted this land.

At the time of Fort Ross, the fur trapper, Michael LaFramboise, explored the Mattole country and came away empty-handed. Even today, the region supports only a handful of permanent residents.

The scattered Mattole ranchers seem no less tradition-bound than the Indians who preceded them. They are disturbed by talk of Highway 1 being extended from Rockport to link with the Redwood Highway near Ferndale. Should this happen, they fear the charm and quiet of their countryside would be shattered by

17

a flood of traffic and commercial development. Land values would soar but so would taxes. Many of the old families practice ranching more as a way of life than as a business.

From the junction at Four Corners, it's five miles by way of the unpaved Chamise Mountain Road to Wailaki Camp on the east slope of the King Range. Here there's a picnic area and twelve campsites on the South Fork of Bear Creek. A short piece up the road is Nadelos Camp, with four sites. These BLM camps have the same improvements as National Forest camps, with benches, tables, food lockers, piped water, stoves, and rest rooms.

From Wailaki Camp, a steep but well-engineered trail switchbacks up Chamise Mountain. The first quarter-mile is signed with BLM markers which identify the native flora. These include many plants and understory trees associated with the redwoods but virtually all the tall timber in the King Range is Douglas fir.

It's slightly better than a mile to the brushy summit at 2,500 feet. From here, you obtain a dazzling view of the Primitive Coast if you're fortunate to make the hike on a fog-less day in Spring.

The trail down the west slope is less developed. It affords a rough four-mile backpack to an isolated beach at the mouth of Chamise Creek.

About a third of the way down, you enter a Gothic belt of forest which drips with condensed fog most days in summer. Douglas firs grow differently here than on the east slope. They loom grotesquely in the mist with their massive trunks twisted and foreshortened so the lower branches sweep the ground.

The trail grows ever more steep and tortuous as you lose elevation.

On the lower edge of the forest where wild iris grow, there are oak-shaded flats suitable for an overnight bivouac. Chamise Creek runs in a ravine to the right of the trail. The BLM map

18

*Rocky beach at mouth of Chamise Creek
invites surf fishing, abalone picking and
prospecting for cockle clams. The only way to
get here is by trail.*

19

shows a dim side trail leading to the stream, but it's good insurance to pack an extra canteen of water.

On its final plunge to the sea, the main trail zig-zags down an open slope, skirting the edge of sea cliffs before it comes out at the mouth of Chamise Creek. The rocky beach here is almost completely covered at high tide. Perch and rockfish are abundant but it's easy to get snagged unless you use a bobber. Abalone picking is good when the sea is calm enough for wading.

This shore is truly isolated. The shallow reefs make it difficult to approach by boat. Two miles north of Chamise Creek, the beach is cut off from Shelter Cove by Point No Pass. Another promontory, also known as Point No Pass, leans to sea three miles south of the creek. The only way out is by trail.

From Wailaki Camp, the Chamise Mountain Road runs north two miles to a junction with the Shelter Cove Road. Turning west, it's a short climb to a pass where we meet the King Range Road at an elevation of 1,996 feet.

The King Range Road is not recommended for trailers. It follows Bear Creek four miles north to Tolkan Camp which has nine sites. About three miles farther is Horse Mountain Camp, also with nine sites. Near this camp, the Saddle Mountain Road takes off up the east slope to the start of Kings Crest Trail. This trail runs nine miles along the summit, climbing 1,000 feet to Kings Peak before it terminates on the north boundary of the BLM property. Several spurs branch off the main trail but none approach the seashore.

The limitations of the BLM trail system may be blamed on the checkerboard pattern of private holdings in the King Range. In 1967, a bill was introduced in Congress which provided for exchange of government and private lands so that the BLM property might be consolidated within a single unit known as the King Range Conservation Area.

*The Pacific slopes of the King Range rise
directly from the sea at angles of 45° or steeper.
This scene was photographed on the
Chamise Mountain trail.*

21

This legislation was stalled when it was proposed that federal land in the King Range be given to California in exchange for the state parks inside the boundaries of the new Redwood National Park. Until this matter is resolved, the trail system is likely to remain pretty much as it is.

From the junction of the Shelter Cove and King Range Roads, it's four miles to the coast at Point Delgada. Near the start of this drive, a weathered sign with peeling paint reads, "Welcome to Shelter Cove—Tomorrow's Vacation Wonderland."

The road emerges from the timber to wind down a grassy mountainside that is laced with a maze of paved streets. The slope has been subdivided into 4,700 lots. Most of the lots have been sold but, as of 1969, only seven homes had been built.

Other improvements include a motel and golf course. At the foot of the grade on the terrace fronting the seashore is Humboldt County's second largest air strip. Separate and apart from the development is a resort at Shelter Cove on the lee side of Point Delgada. Here there's a restaurant, trailer park, launching ramp, bait shop, and boat rentals.

When Shelter Cove was occupied by the Sinkyone, it was a source of clam money for the Northern Pomo. The first white settlement was built around a mill which processed tanbark oak for export to foreign countries.

There was a hotel and several saloons, but the old port was insignificant compared with the scale of the present development. Shelter Cove is still a lonely place. But if and when all the lots are built up with homes and apartments, the subdivision might rival Eureka in population.

According to a brochure supplied by the developer, "The skilled planners of Shelter Cove are making certain its natural beauty will be retained. The greater part of the land is untouched; the colors of nature are visible in every direction. The miles of sea-scented beach will always be accessible to the public and there will be parks along the guardian palisade."

Hopefully, the developers are correct but already there is trouble in Eden.

Since 1965, the roads and utilities at Shelter Cove have been administered by the Resort Improvement District 1 of Humboldt County. The District Board of Directors was elected by the one eligible voter, a representative of the Shelter Cove Company of Los Angeles. In 1969, this board was taken to task by the Humboldt County Grand Jury. No legal action was initiated but the panel recommended an expert evaluation of "deficiencies and overpayment made to the contractor-developer."

Early in 1970, a firm of engineering consultants hired by the county estimated it would cost $1,870,600.00 to correct or repair the roads and drains. The estimate did not include shortcomings noted in the sewer and water systems.

Often fog-bound in summer, the main attractions at Shelter Cove are beachcombing, skin diving, and sport fishing. Many old hands believe Shelter Cove is the finest salmon port on the North Coast. The trolling grounds lie close inshore on the shoals off Point Delgada. A fair number of king salmon are hooked but the bulk of the catch is silvers.

Bottom fishing is excellent for lingcod, cabezon, and black, blue, copper, and vermillion rockfish. Halibut in excess of 50 pounds have been caught. The rocky shore around Point Delgada abounds with tidepools and affords good casting for rockfish. Some fine abalone beds become accessible to waders on extreme minus tides.

The black sand beaches which stretch north and south of the peninsula yield driftwood, cockle clams, and a few agates. Perch and smelt are taken in the surf. The water here is normally too cold and rough for swimming.

*Ettersburg is a ranch settled by Albert F. Etter
in 1894. Apples were shipped from here by horse
and wagon to a schooner landing at mouth
of the Mattole River.*

CHAPTER 17: CAPE MENDOCINO Cape Mendocino's primitive coast is not entirely roadless. Near the Eel River, it's touched by the Centerville Road out of Ferndale. The Mattole Road skirts four miles of low, sandy seashore on the south side of the Cape.

To approach the Cape from Shelter Cove, the traveler may proceed north by way of the King Range or Ettersburg Roads. Neither of these steep, unpaved byways is recommended for trailers. Both run about eleven miles to connect with the Wilder Ridge Road at the foot of Kings Peak. Eight miles north from here, the Wilder Ridge Road meets the Mattole Road at Honeydew.

The Ettersburg Road branches off the Shelter Cove Road about midway between Garberville and Point Delgada. Logging trucks use this slender ridge route which winds above the Mattole River across a patchwork quilt of forest and meadow. It's a six-mile drive to Ettersburg where the road dips to span the river.

Ettersburg is not a town but a private ranch with an air strip. It was settled in 1894 by Albert F. Etter who established an experimental fruit farm here. Apples grown on the ranch were delivered by horse and wagon to a schooner landing at the mouth of the Mattole River.

The Mattole River flows north from Ettersburg through wild country. The road bears west five miles to a junction with the King Range and Wilder Ridge Roads. At an elevation of 2,224 feet, this lonely crossroads affords a good overall view of the King Range and its loftiest peaks.

The Wilder Ridge Road contours through timber and open range, gradually losing altitude as it approaches the Mattole River at Honeydew. Along the way are several stock ranches with charming old homes. The drive is especially pleasing in

Time has softened some of the scars left by logging in the Mattole River Country.

Spring when the hillsides are bright with white and purple fox-gloves.

Honeydew used to be a fair-sized town when it was an active lumber center. Now there's only a post office and two small stores with gas pumps. The paved Mattole Road, which is also known as the Wild Cat Road, crosses the river here and winds 23 miles northeast to join US Highway 101 in Humboldt Redwoods State Park.

During the winter of 1957-58, Honeydew received 174 inches of rain.

On the west side of town the remains of an old saw mill are visible. A short way further is a coffee shop which is followed by two rustic resorts with cabins, trailer spaces, and camp sites.

From Honeydew, it's fifteen miles to Petrolia. On this stretch, the road follows the river. At a few points, the pavement dips low and close enough to the stream to afford fishing access. Winter steelheaders work this water with bait beginning in late December.

Both king and silver salmon enter the river after winter rains open the sand bar at the mouth. There's summer angling for pan-sized trout in some of the tributaries. But along most of its 50-mile course, the Mattole is a private preserve. A state survey shows public access to be only one per cent of the steelhead water and no public access to good salmon water.

The Mattole ranchers, in recent years, have been less disposed to grant strangers permission to hunt and fish on their property. They complain that too many recreationists are litter bugs and tend to be careless about such things as closing stock gates.

The Mattole is named for a tribe of Athabascan Indians who had several villages in the vicinity of Cape Mendocino. They

The Mattole River near Petrolia; the countryside is blend of hayfields, apple orchards, brushland, and second-growth forest.

shared the fate of the neighboring Sinkyone before scholars could learn much about them.

The hilly countryside off the river is a blend of hayfields, apple orchards, brushland, and second-growth forest. Time has softened the scars left by fire and clear cutting. Some logging continues but on a smaller scale.

Eight miles west of Honeydew on the Mattole Road is a privately operated campground and trailer park.

Petrolia is a drowsy place which sprawls across the lower slopes of Apple Tree Ridge. A steepled church and wooden school house with a bell tower lend charm to the village. There are two rustic motels and a single store with a gas pump.

Settlement came in 1861 when oil was discovered in the hills a few miles north of town. The first producing oil wells in California were drilled here. Of these, the most successful was the Union Well drilled by the Mattole Petroleum Company of which Leland Stanford was president. It yielded about 100 barrels of oil at the rate of one barrel a day.

In later years, derricks sprouted at Honeydew, the Etter Ranch, and near Briceland. None of these produced more than a token amount of oil.

A post office was established at Petrolia in 1865. It was during this year the first shipment of oil was made. One hundred gallons in goatskin bags was packed out by mule train.

In 1871, a stage road from Ferndale was completed to Petrolia by the Petrolia and Centerville Plank and Turnpike Company. This road was gradually extended to Garberville along portions of the routes now followed by the Mattole, Wilder Ridge, Ettersburg, and Shelter Cove Roads. From Garberville, a road climbed to link with the Mail Ridge Road in the Eastern Highlands. Before the Usal Road was built, the Mail Ridge Road provided the only overland approach to San Francisco.

The lagoon inside the mouth of the Mattole River is approached on a side road which forks off the Mattole Road near the bridge crossing east of town. This spur is known as the Lighthouse Road because it connects with a trail leading to the site of the Punta Gorda Light Station. After 39 years of service, the light was abandoned in 1951 and replaced by a whistle buoy anchored at sea.

The lower end of the Lighthouse Road is unpaved, and fit for travel only in a four-wheeled drive vehicle. Fly fishing is sometimes excellent on the lagoon during the first half of the winter steelhead season. The outer beach affords netting for surf smelt as well as perch fishing. Driftwood is abundant and glass fishing floats occasionally turn up.

Leaving Petrolia, the main road spans the North Fork of the Mattole River. On the west bank, the Cooke Road follows the stream north a couple miles to approach the ranch where the site of the first oil well is signed by a state historical marker.

On the thirty-mile drive from Ferndale, there are no towns, resorts, or gas stops. It's four miles over a low grassy ridge to the sand dunes at the mouth of Domingo Creek. Here the road swings north and hugs the shoreline as far as Cape Mendocino.

This is a windy coast that is fog-bound most days in summer.

About halfway to the Cape, there is the Devil's Gate. The road skirts this outcropping on a low, wave-licked causeway which is hazardous to drive in stormy weather.

A lone residence known as the Ocean House looks out on Cape Mendocino where the road veers inland to climb Cape Ridge. Sugarloaf Island is visible from the pavement here. It towers 300 feet above the water just a stone's throw off the point.

Cape Mendocino, being the most westerly point on the Pacific Coast south of Alaska, has served as a landmark for navigators since the 16th Century. Cabrillo may have been the first Euro-

Petrolia.

pean to see the Cape on his voyage of discovery in 1542. Drake, Cermeno, and Vizcaino reported sighting it. It was a landfall for many of the Manila galleons which sailed the Great Circle Route back to New Spain with treasure from the Orient.

On the tip of Cape Ridge, there's an automatic light. The original light was housed in a sixteen-sided pyramidal tower, built in 1868.

Fauntleroy Rock, Blunt's Reef, and The Great Break are among the shoals which accounted for more than 200 shipwrecks off Cape Mendocino in the period from 1850 to 1950.

On a foggy day in June of 1916, the 4,057-ton steamer, Bear, foundered near the Cape. The vessel carried 182 passengers and crew, of whom 155 were rescued. Attempts were made to salvage the Bear but it was a total loss. Captain Dollar's little lumber schooner, the Grace Dollar, was among the ships which picked up survivors.

It was calm and clear on the night of August 6, 1921, when the steamer, Alaska, unaccountably plowed into Blunt's Reef, three miles west of the Cape. Most of the passengers were gathered for a dance when the collision occurred. Forty-two persons were lost.

On the far side of Cape Ridge, the road drops to Capetown, located a mile inland on the Bear River. A former stop on the old toll road, Capetown is headquarters for a sheep ranch. The last excitement was in the 1860's when some oil wells were drilled in Bear Valley. For many years, the cook stove in a farmhouse at Capetown was operated on natural gas obtained from seepage near the bridge crossing.

Bear Valley and the hills to the north have the look of the Scottish Highlands. There are scattered stands of timber, but mostly the rolling slopes support only grass, low brush, and clumps of purple thistle. The roadsides are edged with daisies.

The unpaved Bear River Road leaves Capetown to approach ranches in the upper valley. Ultimately, this road connects with the Bear Ridge Road which runs to Rio Dell.

King salmon, silver salmon, and steelhead rainbow trout enter the Bear River after winter rains open the bar. As with all the smaller rivers, the problem is to arrive on the stream when a run of fish is at its peak. By the time Eureka bait shops receive word of action, the run may be scattered far upstream.

Access for fishing at Bear River is by permission of the land-owner.

From Capetown, which is 45 feet above the sea, the Mattole Road winds to a junction at 1,877 feet on Bunker Hill. The Bear Ridge Road leaves here for Rio Dell. A trifle west of the junction is Oil Creek where several wells were drilled in the 1860's.

The pavement bears north across the northern tip of the Mendocino Highlands, passing through ragged stands of timber and fog-damp meadows that are green with bracken. After six miles, the road comes to a drop-off overlooking the flat, fertile plain of the Eel River Delta.

Nestled at the foot of the grade is the quaint Victorian town of Ferndale.

Winter steelheading on the South Fork of the Eel River near Garberville.

Part VI

The old coastline is steep and timbered. The new coastline is low, sandy, and treeless. It was built up by wave action and the sweep of ocean currents. ¶ Most of the population in Humboldt County lives in the area between the two coastlines. Here are river-built plains, several fresh water lagoons, and Humboldt Bay. ¶ The seashore of the Double Coast extends from the Eel River fifty miles to Redwood Creek. Humboldt Bay has 35 miles of protected shore. ¶ At Fortuna, Eureka, and Arcata, the traveler finds a good selection of restaurants, stores, and overnight accommodations. There's swimming in Big Lagoon and overnight camping at Patrick's Point State Park.

CHAPTER 18: THE EEL RIVER DELTA   The coastal plain of the Eel River Delta invites a full day of road exploring. This bottomland spreads north of Ferndale almost to Humboldt Bay and east to Carlotta where the Van Duzen River first emerges from its wooded canyon.

The Delta plain is dotted with dairy farms and laced with winding waterways, such as Hogpen Slough and the Salt River. There are scattered towns of which the largest are Ferndale, Loleta, Fortuna, and Rohnerville.

Ferndale is less a rural trading center than a sophisticated exurb of Eureka. As one of the best preserved of the pioneer settlements, the town is filled with homes and stores rendered in a modified version of the high Victorian style. Much in evidence are fans, niches, gables, bay windows, cornices, and bracketed eaves replete with elaborate fretwork.

*Steelhead action at Boundary Hole—South Fork
of the Eel River near Benbow Lake.
Photo made on New Year's Day.*

The first settlement was in 1852. At this time, much of the Delta was forested with redwoods. Some trees were said to have stood more than 400 feet tall. The timber was sufficiently cleared for dairy ranching by the 1870's when farmers from Denmark founded the town. Later came settlers of Portuguese and Italian descent.

Main Street is lined with antique shops and art galleries. There's a choice of restaurants but commercial accommodations are limited.

The Centerville Road out of Ferndale runs 4½ miles west to the Centerville Beach County Park. There is a picnic area with restrooms. The park is only four acres but provides access to ten miles of sand beach between False Cape and the Eel River Lagoon.

A quarter-mile south of the picnic area, an historical marker memorializes the wreck of the Northerner in the winter of 1860. This Panama Mail Line steamer was weathering a storm en route to the Columbia River when it ran aground on Blunt's Reef.

The steamer began to sink the instant it was backed off the reef. With pumps removing 12,000 gallons of water a minute, Captain W. L. Dall set a course for Humboldt Bay. But the pumps were not equal to their task. As the vessel was about to founder, the captain steered directly for the beach.

Attempts were made to ferry the 108 passengers ashore by lifeboat. The first boat made it through the breakers. The second boat capsized. Some survivors drifted to safety on sections of the deck. Others were landed by means of a line stretched to the beach. Thirty-eight persons were lost.

Driftwood collectors do well on the Centerville Beach and there's good smelt netting here in summer. Surf casting for redtail perch is apt to be most rewarding after New Year's Day through early summer.

Autumn is a beautiful time of year to go camping at Grizzly Creek Redwoods State Park.

Of several varieties of surfperch hooked off North Coast beaches, the ubiquitous redtail forms the bulk of the catch. This silvery fish has a soup plate configuration with dark vertical bars on its sides and a touch of red in the tail fin. The adults move inshore to spawn from late winter through Spring. They range to 18 inches in length and a maximum of five pounds in weight. Being a "dry" fish, surfperch are best prepared for the table by dipping the fillets in batter and frying briefly at high heat.

Since most North Coast beaches have steep drop-offs, it's rarely necessary to make long casts in order to reach productive water. The rod and reel should be heavy enough for use with 15 pound test line and pyramid sinkers to four ounces. The choice of sinker weight is dictated by the roughness of the surf.

The terminal rig consists of a three-foot leader with a snap on the end for the sinker and one or two droppers for size No. 4, 6, or 8 snelled hooks. Good baits are sand crabs, shrimp, mussels, pileworms, and chunks of fish.

After casting, the sinker is allowed to rest on the bottom. The trick is to keep a taut line so strikes may be detected. Surfperch usually bite best on a running tide.

From Ferndale, it's a short drive by way of Main Street to the Eel River crossing at Fernbridge, a small hamlet built around a creamery. On the east bank, we turn left on Old Highway 101 and proceed two miles north to Loleta, another creamery town.

Most milk produced in the Delta is processed into butter and dried powders. The big urban markets for the more profitable Grade A milk are too remote. Presently, there's talk of cultivating Delta pasture for vegetable production. If this happens, the price of hay will go up. But recent changes in the state milk marketing agreement and further extension of the US 101 freeway may allow some Delta farmers to sell more Grade A milk.

The Copenhagen Road out of Loleta bears north through lush

*Victorian fronts of stores in Ferndale are
painted in striking combinations of pastel colors.*

grazing land to approach Table Bluff, a low ridge which divides Humboldt Bay from the Delta. At the junction with the Table Bluff Road, we turn left and climb the ridge to obtain our first view of the bay.

About 14 miles long and up to 3½ miles wide, Humboldt Bay is the only major embayment left on the California Coast with miles of shoreline in their natural state. The bay remains sufficiently free of pollution to permit oyster farming. Eureka residents seem determined to keep their bay unspoiled. A proposal to create a National Wildlife Refuge on the bay has strong local support. The refuge would encompass 9,350 acres, or 71 per cent of the bay, including open water, mud flats, and salt marshes.

The Table Bluff Road winds by an Indian settlement and an old light station before it drops down on the sandy South Spit. At the foot of the bluff, there's an undeveloped county beach known as Clam Park. The best clamming here is on the bay side of the spit on tidal flats which yield softshell, little neck, gaper, and Washington clams.

The crude shelters seen spaced across the flats are used as blinds by duck hunters. Some of the best shooting comes in the season for the maritime goose known as the black brant.

Driftwood abounds on the oceanside of the spit, but the breakers here are almost too rough for fishing. The violence of the surf is explained by the sandy shoals offshore. Collectively, these are spoken of as the Humboldt Bar.

A gravel road runs the length of the spit, three miles to the South Jetty. This road is unsafe for travel in winter. In Spring, the sand dunes which crown the spit are aglow with yellow lupines.

When you stand on the jetty to view the slender opening to Humboldt Bay, it may seem credible that this large body of water escaped notice by mariners until the 19th Century. Jonathan

41

Victorian farmhouse on the outskirts of Ferndale.

Winship, a captain employed by the Russian-American Fur Company, entered the bay in 1806. Yet, for practical purposes, it remained undiscovered until Josiah Gregg's eight-man party came overland from the Trinity River in the winter of 1849.

The goal of the Gregg expedition was to locate the mouth of the Trinity River, which is the largest tributary of the Klamath River. At the time, it was widely supposed that the Trinity came out somewhere on the coast.

Josiah Gregg died on the rugged trek to San Francisco. But soon after the emaciated survivors of his party straggled into town, there was a great rush to establish trading posts on "Trinity Bay." Eleven ships and several overland expeditions were hastily outfitted by rival companies who believed the bay had a future as a port for the Northern Mines.

The bay made a satisfactory port except for the treacherous approach across the Humboldt Bar. Scores of ships foundered on the bar in winter storms. Many more came to grief in the pea soup fogs which frequent this coast in summer.

The most spectacular loss occurred in 1917 when a heavy cruiser, the USS Milwaukee, flagship of the Pacific Fleet, was sent to salvage a submarine grounded on the North Spit. When the Milwaukee attempted to winch the submarine off the spit, it was drawn by its own cable onto the beach. Here it remained until dismantled for scrap in World War II.

Captain "Midnight" Olson earned his nickname by crossing the bar on a stormy night when the channel was said to have been twenty feet deep on the crest of the waves and six inches deep in the troughs. The present channel is maintained at a depth of 45 feet.

The channel, where it runs to sea between the North and South Jetties, is not safe for small boats on the outgoing tide. Most any day in Summer when the tide is right the channel will

Table Bluff Road winds down to South Spit on lower Humboldt Bay.

be dotted with small cruisers and outboard-powered skiffs trolling for salmon. King salmon predominate over silvers in the catch here.

Fishing off the South Jetty is good for a variety of fish, including striped sea perch, kelp greenling, and starry flounder. White market crabs, locally known as Dungeness crabs, are taken with ring nets. Jetty fishing invites the use of lighter tackle than is customarily used for casting off the rocks.

Autos are not permitted, but pedestrians may walk nearly a mile out to sea on the South Jetty.

Returning to Loleta, we leave Old Highway 101 on the Cannibal Road which runs 4½ miles west to Mosley Island on the Eel River Lagoon. The road terminates at a county small boat launching area known as Crab Park.

The lagoon and estuary afford trolling for king salmon in October and silver salmon in November or early December. Ring nets are used to trap market crabs during the season which is normally best from late Winter through Spring.

Crabbing is largely a matter of luck. It may take hours of prospecting to find a productive spot. The ring net, baited with fish, is lowered to the bottom with a rope to which a buoy is attached. Low tide is best and the water should be fairly calm. After waiting 10-15 minutes, you haul in the ring net as quickly as possible, taking care not to jar the boat in a way that might spook the crabs.

Angling regulations specify size and creel limits for market crabs and provide for the release of all female crabs. There are no limits or closed season for red rock crabs. The latter are inferior to market crabs in that the edible meat is mostly concentrated in the claws.

Small boats may be launched at Cock Robin Island. The undeveloped county fishing access here is approached on a side

45

Salmon fishing off the South Jetty at the
entrance to Humboldt Bay.

road which leaves the Cannibal Road at a point 2½ miles west of Loleta.

The Eel River, which drains 3,480 square miles of mountain country, holds some of the choicest steelhead water in the West. Old hands may be heard to grumble that the fishing isn't what it used to be. State biologists can cite case after case of damage to the feeder streams by road building and logging pollution. Even so, the Eel is still a great fishing river. A recent survey shows the Eel yields to anglers approximately 3,400 salmon and 13,000 steelhead each season.

Steelhead may enter the Eel as early as July but the peak action occurs in Winter beginning in late November. The river from Fernbridge to the mouth is open to year around fishing. On this stretch are such famous holes as Fulmore, Snag, and Singley Pools. These are mostly worked by skiff fishermen, using bait, flashers, or wet streamer flies, such as the Carson, Shrimp, Mickey Finn, and Golden Demon.

Upstream from Fernbridge are myriad pools and riffles suitable for wading. Some of the best water is found in the State Redwood Parks on the South Fork of the Eel.

Below Loleta near Fernbridge is the interchange for the US 101 freeway. The exit for Fortuna is three miles south.

Fortuna is a residential town which sprawls at the foot of a timbered slope on the eastern edge of the river plain. It was variously known as Springville, Slide, and Fortune when it was settled in the 1870's. Visitors are welcome to tour a cider works, cheese factory, and plywood plant. There are numerous motels and restaurants.

Right next door to Fortuna is an older settlement known as Rohnerville. It was founded in 1859 by Henry Rohner, a native of Switzerland.

The old Mail Ridge route, mentioned earlier in this guide,

47

affords a fascinating drive. Starting from Fortuna, we take the Rohnerville Road south to Hydesville. Here we turn left on State Highway 36 and follow the Van Duzen River to a junction with the unpaved Alderpoint Road at Bridgeville. The Alderpoint Road links with other back roads to provide a 55-mile drive along the loosely forested crest of Mail Ridge. The drive ends on the Redwood Highway twelve miles north of Laytonville.

On the Van Duzen River, there is Grizzly Redwoods State Park with campsites handy to a good swimming hole. More than half the prime redwoods in this park were acquired in 1969 as a gift from the Georgia-Pacific Corporation. Carlotta and Strong's Station are old settlements on the river with one foot still in the past.

Ferndale is filled with relics of the past.
This hitching post stands on sidewalk off Ocean
Avenue between Berding and Main Streets.

CHAPTER 19: EUREKA Of eleven vessels which left San Francisco in the Spring of 1850 to pioneer a port for the Northern Mines, the first to sight Humboldt Bay was the schooner, Laura Virginia, commanded by Douglas Ottinger.

It was probably Ottinger who named the bay in honor of the naturalist-explorer, Alexander von Humboldt. But when Ottinger's first mate, Hans Henry Buhne, entered the harbor in a small boat, the great race had only begun. There were years of fierce competition between rival ports before the winner was declared.

Driving north on US 101, the first town on the bay is Fields Landing which didn't appear on the map until the 1890's. The settlement is clustered around the Olson Terminal and Pacific Lumber Company docks. There's a small boat launching ramp at the foot of Railroad Avenue.

Just north of Fields Landing, a side road runs to Buhne Point. This drive approaches California's first privately financed atomic power plant. Before the facility was built, Eureka obtained much of its power and light from the Donbass III, a salvaged Russian tanker which was towed into the bay and beached in 1946.

On the tip of Buhne Point is a development known as King Salmon. Here are several fishing resorts with trailer space, skiff rentals, and launching facilities. Charter boats and scheduled party boats operate from here in summer.

The partyboats troll a short distance outside the bay for king and silver salmon. Usually, it's no more than a 20-minute trip to the fishing grounds. Tackle may be rented at the boat landing.

Cannonball sinkers up to 1½ pounds are used with a device which releases the weight when a salmon strikes the bait. Torpedo sinkers as light as three ounces may suffice in late summer when the salmon begin to bunch up off the river mouths. At this time, the fish are more prone to forage near the surface.

The frontage north of Buhne Point to the Eureka city limit was the site of Humboldt City, the earliest settlement on the bay. It was founded by Douglas Ottinger on April 14, 1850. The town faded quickly because it was located too far south to compete in the trade with the Klamath mines.

Ottinger's associate, Hans Henry Buhne, eventually settled on Buhne Point after experience as a miner, merchant, harbor pilot, whaling master, and professional deer hunter. He made his fortune as part owner of the largest saw mill on the bay.

Three miles north of Fields Landing, the highway spans the Elk River, named by the Gregg party after it enjoyed a dinner of elk near the stream. Two spurs leading off the Elk River Road span the creek on antique covered bridges. Roosevelt elk still roam the wild country at the headwaters.

A mile farther we enter Eureka on Broadway. This corner of the city was formerly the town of Bucksport. It was founded in the summer of 1850 by David Buck, a survivor of the Gregg expedition.

On a bluff overlooking the Bucksport district is the Fort Humboldt State Historical Monument. It is approached by way of Fort Avenue. An old commissary building still stands. There's a museum and exhibit of early logging apparatus.

Fort Humboldt was garrisoned from 1853 until 1870 to protect the settlers from the Indians. There were many minor skirmishes, one of the last taking place at Chalk Mountain near Bridgeville on the Van Duzen River. The fort is chiefly remembered because Ulysses S. Grant was stationed at it. Grant, depressed by his assignment, drank heavily. After six months, he resigned his commission and rejoined his family at St. Louis where he briefly tried his hand at farming.

US 101 follows Broadway through "Motel Row" to approach the waterfront in the northwest corner of the city. At the foot of

A sand shark is hooked off pier at Eureka Boat Basin where many commercial fishing craft are based.

*The Carson Mansion has 18 rooms ornamented
with rare woods imported from South America.*

Commercial Street is a basin where most of Eureka's fleet of 450 commercial fishing boats is based. There's a small boat launching ramp.

Visitors are welcome to tour the plants of the Lazio Fish Cannery at the foot of "C" Street and the Coast Oyster Company at the foot of "A" Street. A passenger ferry to Samoa on the North Spit operates from the foot of "F" Street.

A bridge to the North Spit is scheduled for completion in 1972. One leg of the span will stand on Gunther Island, named for a settler who dyked its banks in order to grow hay. Hans Henry Buhne went into partnership to build a lumber mill on the island in 1865. Presently, the island is a picnic spot, deserted except for the herons, egrets, and Western clapper rails which frequent its marshy shoreline. The adjoining mud flats yield gaper, geoduck, and Washington clams.

Artifacts have been unearthed at Gunther Island which suggest Indian occupation for more than 1,000 years. After a party of settlers raided a Wiyot village here to slaughter 100 women and children, Bret Harte wrote a scathing editorial in the Arcata newspaper, "The Northern California." Harte was then a "printer's devil" who had temporarily taken charge while the editor was absent. For siding with the Indians, he was hounded out of town.

In 1885, when there were few Indians left, the citizens found occasion to vent their wrath against the city's Chinese population. All the Chinese were evacuated and their property confiscated following the accidental shooting of a city councilman in a "tong war."

US 101 North leaves Broadway at Fifth Street to run east through the business district. Here a facade of modern store fronts and some new public buildings give Eureka the look it should have as the principal trading center for Humboldt and

53

*William Carson built this house as a wedding
present for his eldest son.*

Del Norte Counties. Yet much of the downtown area appears shabby and run down. There's a skid row near the waterfront.

The term "skid row" is said to have originated on the North Coast. It referred to the shanty towns which sprang up alongside the early skid roads where they terminated at a coastal mill.

A Boston contractor named James T. Ryan was the prime mover of the Mendocino Company which founded Eureka in May of 1850. Some accounts have Ryan leaping ashore from a whale boat to shout, "Eureka!," which is Greek for "I have found it." Ryan went on to become a wealthy lumberman, state senator, and general of the Northern California militia.

For a time, Eureka lagged behind neighboring Arcata which was better situated on the trail to the Northern Mines. Eureka was positioned at the head of deep water navigation on the bay. This advantage proved decisive when lumber exports became more important than trade with the mines. In 1856, the county seat shifted from Arcata to Eureka.

Eureka is probably best known outside the Redwood Empire as the "coolest city in the nation." This only applies in summer; the average temperatures in July are 52 degrees minimum and 60.7 degrees maximum. In January, the range is 41.1 minimum and 53.6 maximum. Average rainfall is 38.43 inches. It's a rare day in summer when the coastal fog lifts to provide an hour or two of sunshine.

"The most photographed house in the nation" is the Carson Mansion located at the foot of "M" Street. Built in 1884, this three-story palace of redwood displays the ultimate in carpenter's Gothic. It's now a headquarters for the exclusive Ingomar Club. Across the street is the Carson House built by William Carson as a wedding gift for his eldest son.

William Carson drifted in from the gold fields and leased a mill on the bay in 1856. Carson was probably the first to fall

*Red rock crabs abound off the county small boat
launching ramp on the North Spit.*

and saw the redwood giants which shaded Eureka down to the waterfront.

The earliest mill was the little "Taupoos" founded in 1850 by Jim Eddy and Martin White just four months after James Ryan founded the town. In 1852, Ryan went into partnership with James Duff to build a large mill. The machinery ordered from San Francisco was swept off the deck of the "Santa Clara" in a storm. So Ryan ordered the vessel beached at a place between "D" and "E" streets. Here the ship's engines were removed and used to power the new mill.

The first shipments of lumber from the Ryan and Duff Mill were lost when the brig, Clifford, and the bark, Cornwallis, foundered on the Humboldt Bar.

William Carson suffered reverses before he went into partnership with William Dolbeer, inventor of the donkey engine which revolutionized logging on the North Coast.

Now most of the old firms are gone. They have been replaced by a handful of corporate giants which have their headquarters outside the state. One holdover is the Pacific Lumber Company. This firm traces its beginning to a small mill built by McPherson and Wetherby on the Albion River in 1869.

Just a block from the Carson Mansion is the plant of the Eureka Oyster Farms which produces a vitamin product derived from oysters. Visitors are welcome to tour the facility.

Humboldt Bay accounts for 90 per cent of the Pacific oysters grown in California.

Recently, 250 acres of oyster beds were ruled off limits for harvesting because of effluent emanating from a nearby residential area. About 600 pollution outlets are reported on the bay. This is not remarkable compared with San Francisco Bay but the local government seems determined to curb all harmful discharges. In 1968, the North Coast Regional Water Quality

Japanese freighter loads lumber at Samoa docks of the Georgia-Pacific Corporation.

Control Board ruled the huge industrial complex of the Georgia-Pacific Corporation must keep effluent out of the bay.

Lumber is still king at Eureka. It provides the bulk of employment and almost everyone depends on it, directly or indirectly. But the industry faces a period of retrenchment as the last prime redwoods are harvested. When there are only tree farms to log, some mills will close and others will be forced to scale down production. With this in mind, the merchants and civic leaders are showing greater independence than heretofore.

Efforts to lure other industry to Eureka have been largely frustrated by the city's isolation from the major centers of population. So the trend is to encourage more tourism and outdoor recreation. This necessarily implies more concern for the condition of the bay, which the city fathers recognize as their greatest natural asset.

Eureka's population rose from 23,000 in 1950 to 29,000 in 1960. By all estimates, the 1970 census will show no dramatic increase.

Sequoia Park's 46 acres located at "W" and Manzanita Streets in the southeast corner of the city hold a remnant of the virgin forest that once ringed Humboldt Bay. There's a small zoo with lions and tigers. The park provided a setting for Peter B. Kyne's "Valley of the Giants," a saga of violence and double dealing in the redwood industry. The novel is based on the conflicts which erupted after rival interests had acquired huge tracts of public land in violation of the Homestead Act of 1862.

A landmark in the city is the Eureka Inn built in the 1920's with a facade of beams and stucco in the Elizabethan style. The Clarke Museum at Third and E Streets is filled with Indian artifacts, old guns, antiques, stuffed birds, and other memorabilia of the early days.

From Eureka, the US 101 freeway curves around the upper

bay to Arcata, known as Uniontown when it was founded on April 17 of 1850. The business district is centered on "The Plaza," where the pack trains assembled to load supplies for the Klamath mines. L. K. Wood, who logged the hardships suffered by the Gregg expedition, headed the thirty-man group which settled the town.

Arcata's pride is Humboldt State College, perched on the lower slopes of a timbered ridge known as Fickle Hill. Some of the nation's first pollution bio-analysts were educated here. The major emphasis is on fisheries, forestry, and oceanography. A recent project of the college is an experimental fish farm intended to establish migratory runs of brown trout, cutthroat trout, steelhead, and silver salmon in Humboldt Bay.

Adjoining the college is the 600-acre Community Forest, laced with trails built by students. This preserve and a twenty-acre enclave known as Redwood Park may be approached at 14th and Bayview Streets.

West of Arcata, the Samoa Road runs out on the North Spit. It's five miles to Manila, a lumber center. Three miles farther is Samoa, an old company town. Here sprawls a vast complex of pulp, veneer, saw, and planing mills which adjoin the docks and lumber yards of the Georgia-Pacific Corporation. The corporation's Samoa Cookhouse is open to the public. The town was founded by John Vance who built a mill and steamer landing here in the 1890's.

The names Manila and Samoa were inspired by the resemblance of Humboldt Bay to Manila Bay and Pago Pago.

Another two miles up the road is Fairhaven where Hans Bendixsen started a shipyard in 1865. More than 100 vessels were launched, including barks, barkentines, and many steam schooners. Presently, Fairhaven is occupied by the towering mills of the US Plywood Corporation and the Crown-Simpson Pulp

Slash burner of McNord Lumber Company at Blue Lake. Flat car stands on a spur of the "Annie and Mary" Railroad.

Company. The pulp mills give rise to a sour odor which may be detected in Eureka when the wind is right.

Some of the larger mills provide guided tours. Information on these may be obtained from the Greater Eureka Chamber of Commerce, located at 2112 Broadway in Eureka.

A mile beyond Fairhaven is a county fishing access with parking space, rest rooms, and launching ramps. The tip of the North Spit is occupied by the Coast Guard.

The mills on the North Spit are served by the Northwestern Pacific Railroad which runs south by way of the Eel River Valley to San Francisco Bay. At Arcata, the line is joined by the tracks of the Arcata and Mad River Railroad. This is the oldest operating railway on the coast. It was founded in 1854 as the Union Wharf and Plank Walk Company. The first rolling stock consisted of a four-wheel cart drawn by an old horse known as "Spanking Fury." It ran on wooden rails from Arcata to the waterfront.

The name was changed in 1881 a few years after the line was extended along the Mad River with narrow gauge steel rails. Affectionately known as the "Annie and Mary Railroad," the company operates a steam-powered excursion train on weekends and holidays in summer. Departures are from the old lumber camp at Blue Lake. To get there, we exit from US 101 two miles north of Arcata and proceed seven miles east on State Highway 299.

Two miles east of US 101 interchange, there's an exit to the North Bank Road which approaches Azalea State Reserve. This 30-acre natural area has picnic tables and 1½ miles of self-guiding nature trails. May is best to see the azaleas in flower.

On the Arcata Bottoms west of town, rural roads approach the Mad River Slough which affords duck hunting and the 92-acre Mad River County Park where smelt netting is good.

The Mad River owes its name to an argument which broke out when the Gregg expedition forded the stream. Josiah Gregg wanted to stop for an instrument reading. The others were anxious to push ahead.

Steelhead and king salmon enter the Mad River after winter rains open the sand bar. There's good summer trout fishing upstream off State Highway 36 and at Ruth Reservoir. A new state hatchery on the river is scheduled to begin operating in 1971. It's expected to produce 700,000 yearling steelhead a year.

*Fisherman on Luffenholtz Beach works dip net
for night smelt.*

CHAPTER 20: TRINIDAD   On this drive, the Redwood Highway rarely strays far from the ocean or ventures close to any significant stand of redwoods. There are some stretches of new freeway which avoid the immediate shoreline. But where these occur, the old by-passed sections of US 101 afford scenic side trips, free from the press of traffic.

After crossing the Mad River, the freeway slices through McKinleyville, a residential community which prides itself as the fastest growing town on the coast. In the decade 1950 to 1960, the population rose from 200 to 5,000. Much of this increase took place at the expense of Eureka.

Just four miles up the highway from McKinleyville, the old company town of Crannel was reported being "phased out" in 1969.

The exit to Crannel provides the best approach to Clam Beach County Park and neighboring Little River State Beach. These undeveloped beaches afford good digging for razor clams. However, the competition is keen when thousands of clam enthusiasts gather here on a minus tide in Spring.

A slender, oval-shaped clam with a thin shell, the razor clam prefers beaches with fine sand. It's an elusive mollusk. You must dig rapidly because it takes only seconds for a razor clam to bury itself out of reach.

Middle Clam Beach Lagoon contains cutthroat trout which seem to bite best in early Spring.

Little River State Beach includes half a mile of frontage on the estuary of Little River. Fishermen gather here in late autumn to cast for steelhead, cutthroat trout, and silver salmon. The estuary marks the spot where the Gregg party first arrived on the coast after an arduous journey from Rich Bar on the Trinity River.

Across the mouth of Little River is Moonstone Beach where

65

Partyboats at Trinidad make daily trips in summer for salmon or bottomfish.

the frontage is private. Just north of Moonstone, the coast turns rocky and precipitous.

From the Crannel exit, it's five miles to Trinidad.

The exit at Trinidad connects with a by-passed stretch of Old US 101 which runs along the edge of sea cliffs south to Little River. On this drive is Luffenholtz County Beach, an immensely scenic shore, famed for its rocky tide pools and dip netting for day and night smelt.

A super abundance of food and oxygen accounts for the rich variety of marine life normally found in tide pools. Aside from clams, mussels, barnacles, crabs, and lobsters, the list includes star fish, periwinkles, sea urchins, sand dollars, jelly fish, sea lettuce, sponges, squids, and sea anemones.

State biologists have found that some tide pool areas on the North Coast are in danger of being "studied to death." On a single day, a Fish and Game warden recently counted thirty bus loads of school children gathering specimens from pools in the Duxbury Reef area near Bolinas. Student collectors from the college and universities are also known to exact a heavy toll. After serious depletion, biologists estimate it takes five to ten years for a tide pool to recover its normal quotient of flora and fauna.

Some ecologists are pressing for the establishment of "marine reserves" where collecting would be prohibited. It's been suggested that recreationists should approach tide pooling as a purely visual experience. Sports fishermen are urged to obtain their bait from stores.

A right turn off the Trinidad exit leads to the center of town where there's only a garage and supermarket. The village sits on a bluff overlooking a small but spectacular harbor which is crowded with fishing boats in summer. Linked to the bluff by a low neck of sand is the dome-like rock known as Trinidad Head. It rises 362 feet above the water.

*Skin divers prepare to go spear fishing
in Trinidad Harbor.*

Sebastian Cermeno sighted Trinidad Head in 1595 but didn't come ashore for fear of the rocks which infest the harbor. On June 9, 1775, Don Bruno de Heceta and Juan de la Bodega climbed to the top of the Head to erect a wooden cross on Trinity Sunday. Settlement came in May of 1850 when two of the eleven ships which came north from San Francisco following Gregg's discovery of Humboldt Bay elected to settle Trinidad as a port.

Trinidad was well situated for trade with the mines. For a year or so, it was competitive with the towns on Humboldt Bay. Some estimates place the peak population at 3,000. People began leaving Trinidad after the shift was made to lumbering. The lack of a safe deep water anchorage was chiefly to blame. The port enjoys no protection from winter storms which blow in from the southwest.

Incorporated in 1852, Trinidad is officially recognized as the oldest town on the North Coast. For some years, it was an important whaling station.

On the north side of the village is Trinidad State Beach. There's a picnic area and small beach which affords good fishing for perch and rockfish. Just a few yards offshore is picturesque Pewetole Island.

Humboldt State College has a marine laboratory in town that's open to the public. The aquarium here features exhibits of rock fish and the life in tide pools.

The Harbor Road leads down to a pier and resort at the foot of Trinidad Head. The facilities here include a restaurant, skiff rentals, and a tramway for launching small boats. Commercial boats discharge fish at the pier in summer. There's a landing used by scheduled partyboats which troll for salmon just a few hundred yards outside the harbor.

Silvers predominate over king salmon in the local catch. When the salmon are scarce, the boats turn to drift fishing for black

Campsite at Patrick's Point State Park.

rock cod, lingcod, and other bottomfish. Anglers casting from the pier take cabezon, striped sea perch, and kelp greenling.

A steep, unpaved spur off the Harbor Road climbs to the lighthouse on Trinidad Head. The tower is open to visitors on weekends. The original light station, built in 1871, was relocated to the village where it serves as a memorial to fishermen lost at sea.

The harbor seen from the bluff at night sparkles from the anchor lights of hundreds of fishing boats.

The drive from Trinidad to Patrick's Point is five miles. This stretch of the Redwood Highway favors the shoreline.

Patrick's Point State Park takes in 425 acres of forest and meadow on a steepsided peninsula which was homesteaded by Patrick Began in 1851. The "big trees" here are Sitka spruce with trunks to ten feet in diameter. A few Port Orford cedar are found. Winter rainfall in the neighborhood of 60 inches accounts for the extremely lush undergrowth of huckleberry, azalea, rhododendron, and other shrubs.

More than 100 campsites are located in groves of red alders and shore pines. There's a small museum with Indian artifacts. According to Yurok mythology, the spirit of the porpoises retired to Patrick's Point, known as Sumig, when the world was about to become populated with humans.

The "Ceremonial Rock" rises in the forest off the drive to the Agate Beach parking area. The summit is approached on 88 stone steps. On a clear day, it affords a view of the coast from Cape Mendocino to the mouth of the Klamath River.

Patrick's Point has an elaborate trail system. The longest hike is on the Rim Trail which tunnels through dense undergrowth along the edge of the bluffs. Several spur trails lead down to rocky outcroppings which are productive spots for fishermen.

The most ambitious spur switchbacks to Agate Beach. This

*Rocky Point as seen off the Rim Trail in
Patrick's Point State Park.*

Agates are easy to find at Agate Beach.

lovely sweep of dark sand stretches north to provide a surf-side approach to the parks at Big Lagoon.

Agates are plentiful at Agate Beach. The best prospecting is along the edge of the surf on patches of coarse sand or gravel. The stones are not hard to recognize when wet, being a variety of quartz that is translucent or nearly transparent. Pieces of jade, jaspar, and other gem material occasionally turn up. The beach also yields some fine pieces of driftwood.

After Patrick's Point comes nine miles of low brushy seaboard filled with shallow coastal lagoons. These are freshwater lakes which evolved over the centuries from salt water bays similar to Humboldt Bay. They are dyked from the sea by slender reefs of sand built up as a result of wave action and the drift of ocean currents.

During winter storms, the lagoons are prone to overflow into the ocean. At such times, the lakes become stocked with a variety of fish, including surfperch, flounder, salmon, steelhead, and cutthroat trout. Angling is apt to be slow except for brief periods in the Spring and Fall.

About two miles north of Patrick's Park, an old section of US 101 approaches Big Lagoon, which is 19 feet deep, four miles long, and covers 2,000 acres. Big Lagoon County Park is at the south end of the lake. Improvements include a picnic area, boat launching facility, and a safe swimming beach. The lagoon tends to fill with aquatic growth in summer. The coastal fog keeps water temperatures on the cool side.

Fishing for steelhead and cutthroat is usually best at the extreme north end of the lake. There is shooting in season for black brant and other water fowl.

Due east of the county park across the Redwood Highway on Maple Creek is the Big Lagoon Camp of the Georgia-Pacific Corporation. During deer season, nimrods may obtain permits

Smelt netting at Luffenholtz Beach.

from the company office here to hunt in the hilly timberland which overlooks the lagoon area.

The low spit of sand which forms the west bank of Big Lagoon is part of Dry Lagoon State Park. This 927-acre preserve stretches north to the shores of Stone Lagoon. On Big Lagoon, the state beach duplicates the facilities of the county park. There's no camping. Agates, driftwood, and perch fishing are main attractions on the ocean side of the spit.

Dry Lagoon is a small marshy basin crowded between Big and Stone Lagoons.

Stone Lagoon is 15 feet deep and covers 521 acres. Part of it lies inside the boundaries of the new Redwood National Park. Rainbow trout are most numerous in the lake.

From Stone Lagoon, the main highway veers across the Gyon Bluffs to travel the sand spit which dykes Freshwater Lagoon. This lake, which runs a trifle smaller than Stone Lagoon, is less prone to spill its banks in winter. It contains rainbow, cutthroat, and Eastern brook trout.

The east shores of Big, Stone, and Freshwater Lagoons lie within The Three Lagoons Recreation Area of the Georgia-Pacific Corporation. It's open to the public for boating, swimming, and fishing.

Just where the Redwood Highway bends inland north of Freshwater Lagoon, a spur leads to Redwood Creek County Park. There's beach access and fishing on the stream for cutthroat, steelhead, and salmon after the first big storm of autumn opens the bar.

Part VII

This splendid coast takes in 75 miles of seashore, of which 33 miles are enclosed by the Redwood National Park, established October 2, 1968. ¶ The new park links several state parks with a large block of forest on Redwood Creek east of Orick. It may be years before the park will function as a single administrative unit. The present boundaries are ill-defined and negotiations for acquisition of the land are still in progress. The state parks continue to operate as before and provide the only developed camps and recreation facilities. ¶ The Redwood Coast is blessed with two great fishing streams, the Smith and Klamath Rivers. On the estuaries of these rivers and at Crescent City, there are restaurants and overnight accommodations. There is camping in three State Redwood Parks.

CHAPTER 21: PRAIRIE CREEK STATE PARK   Within a few years, the Redwood Highway, where it rolls through Prairie Creek State Park, faces the prospect of becoming a modern freeway or a quiet parkway. Hopefully, the latter will prevail because the former would seriously damage the park.

The effect of freeway construction in Humboldt Redwoods State Park was the removal of thousands of trees, including many ancient redwoods. The massive cuts and fills disrupted the natural pattern of drainage in a way that threatens the health of the big trees which line the Avenue of the Giants. The latter road is a bypassed section of Old US 101 which winds through some of the most impressive redwood groves on the Eel River. Nowhere on this lovely drive is it possible to escape the sound of traffic on the freeway.

The county road to Gold Bluffs Beach winds through patches of virgin forest.

The US 101 freeway was originally planned to pass through a number of the largest redwood parks because they provided the cheapest, most direct routing. Only a concerted stand by the Save-the-Redwoods League, the Sierra Club, and other groups achieved a temporary moratorium on building a freeway through Prairie Creek State Park. Several alternative routes have been proposed, of which only one would not harm the park. This would run east of the park, out of sight and hearing across logged-over land.

Encompassing sixteen square miles of virgin forest, Prairie Creek is the crowning gem of the state preserves north of Eureka. Here, the redwood giants march down to a spectacular seashore where elk roam. The dense summer fogs and up to 100 inches of winter rain support a ground cover which approaches the lushness of the Olympic Rain Forest.

The undergrowth includes a huge diversity of mosses, lichens, liverworts, ferns, and shrubs. Botanists have catalogued 500 kinds of mushrooms and 800 varieties of flowers. Competing with the redwoods for space are lowland firs, Douglas firs, western hemlocks, and Sitka spruce.

Park headquarters and over 100 campsites are located off US 101 bordering a large meadow known as "The Prairie." Most of the park is primitive, in no way altered except for a network of trails with a combined length of 29 miles. Aside from the Redwood Highway, there are two park drives. The Cal Barrel Road skirts the east boundary of the park. The Davidson-Ossagon Roads afford access to Gold Beach.

The park grew to its present size of 13,000 acres chiefly through contributions of land by the Save-the-Redwoods League.

Approaching the park from Freshwater Lagoon, we enter the valley of Redwood Creek. Here the scars left by logging are clearly evident on the hillsides. We soon come to Orick, a small

Roosevelt elk graze the dunes at
Gold Bluffs Beach in early morning and evenings.

ranching and lumbering center with a motel, restaurant, and several stores.

North of town 1½ miles, the Bald Hills Road points east to wind 23 miles across rugged mountains to Martin's Ferry on the Klamath River. The first twelve miles are paved. About nine miles up the road, a dim lane approaches the start of a 4½-mile hike to the "world's tallest trees." This grove in the canyon of Redwood Creek is topped by the Howard Libby Redwood which crests at 367.8 feet. The grove was in the path of timber cutting when it was discovered by an expedition of the National Geographic Society in 1963.

The primeval forest on Redwood Creek and neighboring Lost Man Creek compose the largest stand of old-growth redwoods in the National Park which did not previously enjoy the protection of a state park. The area is roadless except for a few rough spurs. Information on access may be obtained at the field office of the National Park Service in Orick.

On the Redwood Highway from the Bald Hills turn-off, it's 1½ miles to the Davidson Road which runs four miles to Gold Beach. Two miles farther is a county fish hatchery where visitors are welcome. It's situated at the confluence of Prairie and Lost Man Creeks. From here, it's 2½ miles to the main campground in Prairie Creek State Park. If you're hauling a trailer, this is a good place to leave it while you visit Gold Beach.

The Davidson Road is a narrow, winding gravel drive which is subject to temporary closure in wet weather. For a short distance, this road passes some enchanting forest in the watershed of Skunk Cabbage Creek. The latter is not part of the National Park and, at last report, was being logged. In 1970, there was legislation pending that would annex the area to the park but it was questionable whether Congress would act in time.

On another stretch of the Davidson Road, we encounter a

Bull elk near Fern Canyon. The 11,000-acre Madison Grant Forest and Elk Refuge is contained within the boundaries of Prairie Creek State Park.

bleak expanse of ragged ridges littered with skid roads and burned stumps. The area is signed, "Arcata Redwood Company—Tree Farm—seeded 1962."

Photographs of this area made shortly after it was logged were circulated by conservation groups to demonstrate the need for a National Park. In the Spring of 1969, new growth was just beginning to hide some of the scars.

Most tree farms on the North Coast are cut selectively in a way that minimizes damage to the watershed and allows for "multiple use." The Arcata Redwood Company elected to clear cut on the principle that, by removing all trees and competitive ground cover, the seedlings would grow at a faster rate. Experiments have shown that, in some areas, this method achieves a good yield of timber.

The main argument against clear cutting is the harm it does to the watershed. The total absence of ground cover, even though temporary, enormously accelerates the process of erosion with disastrous effect on the streams.

In the bitter controversy that grew out of the campaign for a National Park, a great deal of nonsense was flung about. For example, there were charges the park was a "red plot." But the more responsible opposition tried to influence the public on the issue of tree farms.

Industry spokesmen claimed no substantial amount of old-growth redwoods could be spared for a park without harm to the local economy. They said the remaining 250,000 acres of prime forest were needed to keep the mills going until the tree farms were ready to support lumbering on a sustained yield basis.

The first official tree farms were not established in the redwood belt until the late 1940's. From 70 to 80 years are required to grow a commercial stand of redwoods. On an average, the trees

*The access road at Gold Bluffs Beach
fords several streams. This is Home Creek.*

grow 2-3 feet the first year, 50 feet in twenty years, 160 feet and 2-3 feet in diameter in seventy years.

The pro-park forces charged the lumbermen on the Redwood Coast had shown little interest in tree farms before the campaign for a park had gathered strength. It was alleged the redwoods were being cut at a rate 2½ times the rate of renewal. The Sierra Club pointed out that a park of 90,000 acres would have virgin timber amounting to less than 1½% of the original forest and would leave 94% of the forest in private hands.

Surveys showed the park would effect a serious loss of employment in Del Norte County. Estimates varied from several hundred to more than a thousand jobs. But a study by the Department of Interior indicated that, after ten years, there would be more employment with a park than without it.

Many North Coast residents opposed the park because it would reduce the revenue from property taxes. Yet the method of taxation was self-defeating in that it was largely to blame for the accelerated cut of old-growth redwoods. California law provides that, after a stand of timber is logged, the landowner may be entitled to forty years or more of tax relief.

As it was finally achieved, the 58,000-acre National Park was a partial victory for the redwood industry. It removed only 10,876 acres of old-growth forest from private holdings. But, in its wake, the park dispute left many issues unresolved.

It's still a question how many firms may pull out after the last prime redwoods are logged. Will tree farming on the rugged North Coast be competitive with lumbering elsewhere? Can second-growth redwood compete with Douglas fir? Does the "boom" in mobile homes signify a shrinking market for lumber? Will the Redwood Park draw the expected flood of visitors? The decade just beginning should provide some answers.

The Davidson Road comes out on the coast near a small

*Driftwood, razor clams, surf casting, and dip
netting for smelt draw visitors to
Gold Bluffs Beach.*

lagoon. From here, it's possible to hike south down the beach to the mouth of Redwood Creek. The beach road runs north through dunes and meadows in the shadow of the Gold Bluffs. These heights are crowned with magnificent firs and redwoods.

From the lagoon, it's 1½ miles to the Gold Bluffs Picnic Area inside the boundaries of Prairie Creek State Park. One-half mile farther is a new 25-site campground bordering the beach at Squashan Creek. The more exposed sites are sheltered from the sea breezes by improvised windbreaks of driftwood. There are benches, tables, piped water, fireplaces, and wash rooms.

The traveler is likely to see elk grazing alongside the beach on the 1½-mile drive from camp to Fern Canyon. Park rangers advise it isn't safe to approach these animals too closely. They are in no way domesticated and roam the park at will.

The original range of the Roosevelt, or Wapiti, elk was from British Columbia to San Francisco Bay. The bulls grow an imposing set of antlers and may attain weight in excess of 700 pounds. During the Autumn rutting season, they are prone to lock horns in combat.

The Prairie Creek elk herds number about 400. Elsewhere on the coast, there are herds on the upper reaches of Elk River and Little River and in Bear Valley of Del Norte County.

A signed trail follows Home Creek into Fern Canyon. Although there are many beautiful "Fern Canyons" on the North Coast, this one is probably the most spectacular. The canyon walls are not high but they are sheer and completely covered with ferns. These include lady, sword, deer, chain, bracken, and five-fingered ferns and the licorice ferns which were used by the early settlers to flavor tobacco.

The white pebbly floor of the canyon affords an easy walk. Here and there, the moss-covered trunk of a fallen giant leans across the creek. One-half mile from the road, the trail climbs

*The sheer walls of Fern Canyon are covered
with many varieties of ferns.*

out of the canyon to link with the James Irvine Trail. This popular footpath runs four miles through the forest to park headquarters off the Redwood Highway.

The beach road fords a broad shallow crossing on Home Creek. From the creek, it's hardly a mile to Gold Dust Falls, a slender cascade which drops 100 feet down the bluff. Three miles further is Ossagon Creek. From here, it's one mile to US 101 on a steep, rough road not recommended for low-slung cars in summer or anything but a jeep during the rainy season.

Gold Beach stretches eleven miles. Surf smelt, redtail perch, razor clams, and driftwood are its main attractions. The dunes fronting the beach are carpeted with wild strawberries.

On this lonely shore, a tent city sprang up in 1851. The occasion was the discovery of gold by five prospectors who wandered down from the Klamath River in the Spring of 1850. A California Division of Mines publication describes how the gold was obtained.

"The success of the operation was dependent on what was known as a 'panning sea.' Waves of a certain size and kind excavated natural riffles in the sand of the beach and gold concentrated in these. After the tide had receded, pack mules were taken to the beach, and the sand was packed in sacks. The gold was very finely divided and was recovered by means of the Oregon tom, ordinary tom, and amalgamating plates. Many thousands of dollars of gold was produced in this way; but the gold is no longer concentrated to the same extent. Perhaps the off-shore deposit that was feeding the beach has been exhausted."

*Yurok maidens at Salmon Festival wear costumes
that are over 200 years old.*

CHAPTER 22: THE KLAMATH RIVER A long time ago, Wah-Pec-oo-May-ow, the Great Spirit, told the other spirits he was ready to shape the world. He would put people on it and provide water, rocks, trees, fish, and animals. The spirits were free to choose what they wanted to be.

The spirit Oregos was friendly to people so he became a high rock at the mouth of the Klamath River. It was the function of Oregos to tell the fish when they should enter the river and what route they should follow on their upstream migration.

The fish did not always obey Oregos in every particular, but mainly they followed his direction. And so, each year in the period from February through April, the little smelt known as candlefish would swarm up the Klamath estuary. These fish contained so much oil, the Yurok people found they could use them as candles.

The sea-run cutthroat trout was loath to take orders. But usually he was present in May when the giant sturgeon was spawning in the estuary. The first runs of napooie, or king salmon, would arrive in July. The steelhead would begin to show in August, followed by the silver salmon in September.

When none of these fish were present, the Yuroks could turn to the ocean for sea weed, crabs, mussels, razor clams, redtail perch, starry flounder, and a variety of rockfishes.

This abundance enabled the Yuroks to achieve a civilization that was remarkable for a Stone Age people. They built sturdy houses of redwood and sea-going canoes with sails. The leaders accumulated land, slaves, and other wealth. They used a 13-month calendar and a monetary system based on the tooth-shaped shells of a mollusk known as the dentalium. The shells originated from a particular area of Puget Sound and were acquired from other Indians through trade.

There were no tribes or clans in a formal sense. There were

91

only families grouped in villages where leadership was provided by the wealthiest men. The slaves were poor Indians unable to pay their debts.

The Yuroks had an elaborate system of claims and compensation which covered marriages, births, and deaths, as well as injury to life or property. Wars amounted to occasional feuds between families, or villages. Illnesses were treated by women known as shamans.

Probably the first contact with the "Waugie," or whiteman, was in 1828 when Jedediah Strong Smith's ailing expedition camped near the mouth of the Klamath. The Yuroks provided food and other assistance. But all semblance of friendship ended shortly after five settlers hiked down the coast from Point St. George to explore the river. This happened in 1850. In the same year, the Klamath was overrun by hordes of gold-crazed Forty-Niners who burned several villages, hunted the Indians for sport, and tore up the river bed in a way that halted the runs of fish.

Klamath City sprang up near the river mouth in 1851. The stores and dwellings were grouped around an iron house which served as a refuge when there was trouble with the Indians. The settlement lasted only a year because gold was scarce on the lower river and ships had difficulty navigating the slender entrance to the lagoon. Later, with the advent of the steam schooner, the old Indian village of Requa was developed as a lumber port.

Until 1963, logs were floated out of the Klamath back country in huge rafts guided by tug boats. Now the virgin forest is gone, but logging by fifty small contractors supports a mill of the Simpson Timber Company.

Despite hard use by the miners and loggers, the Klamath River survives as one of the great angling waters of the world. It's

92

Klamath Indians play the stick game with a team from Crescent City.

California's second largest river, 263 miles long, and draining an area of 8,000 square miles. The source is Upper Klamath Lake in south central Oregon. Near the California-Oregon line, the stream is impounded by several power dams. But from Iron Gate Reservoir 188 miles to the mouth, there are no barriers to interfere with the runs of steelhead and salmon.

Of 200 tributaries, the Salmon, Scott, and Trinity Rivers are the largest. These streams and 133 miles of the main river wind through beautiful canyons in the Klamath, Six Rivers, and Shasta-Trinity National Forests. They are closely followed by roads which afford access to hundreds of pools and riffles.

Commercial fishing was outlawed on the Klamath in 1934. But the Indians still work tribal salmon holes, employing the same style of net used by their ancestors for centuries. And from mid-Summer through Autumn, sport fishermen gather by the thousands on the lower river and lagoon. It's estimated about one-fourth of the turn-out is women.

Catering to the angling fraternity are the villages of Requa, Camp Klamath, and Klamath Glen and resorts off the Klamath Beach Road. There is every facility, including campgrounds, trailer parks, motels, lodges, restaurants, bait stores, smoke houses, freezing plants, custom canneries, guide service, skiff rentals, and small boat launching ramps.

Several jet boats based on the lagoon feature scenic cruises on the river. One boat makes a daily run in summer 32 miles upstream to China Creek, with a stopover for lunch at Pecwan in the Hoopa Valley Indian Reservation.

If you're in a hurry to wet a line in the Klamath, the most direct approach from Prairie Creek State Park is by way of the US 101 freeway which resumes on the north boundary of the park.

The by-passed section of US 101, known as the Alder Camp

*This Yurok family home at Requa may be
the oldest dwelling in California.*

Road, affords a more interesting drive. It leaves the main highway just inside the park to skirt the edge of redwood-forested bluffs which crest 500 feet above the sea. About three miles from the park, the road passes within sight of a leaning promontory known as Split Rock. According to Yurok mythology, the great fracture which divides the rock was caused when an Indian anchored his net there and the Spirit of the West Wind filled it with an enormous catch of salmon.

The drive links with the Klamath Beach Road which curves around Flint Ridge overlooking the great gorge where the Klamath meets the sea.

A spur off the Klamath Beach Road leads down to the sand spit which encloses the lagoon. Here the excitement is huge after the salmon runs begin in mid-July. Spin fishermen stand shoulder-to-shoulder on the spit casting spoons, spinners, and bait. Just out of range are the skiff fishermen who troll or "anchor fish" in a manner that permits the current to give action to a fresh anchovy bait.

Occasionally, there are scenes of wild confusion as lines tangle, boats collide, and tempers rise. A Coast Guard vessel is posted near the entrance of the lagoon to keep boats away from "Suicide Row." Skiff fishermen used to anchor gunwale-to-gunwale here within a short distance of the pounding surf. Such is the force of the river current combined with the outgoing tide that a small boat caught up in it is powerless to resist being swept into the breakers.

In recent years, the annual run of king salmon on the Klamath has averaged 168,000 fish. Perch, flounder, and sturgeon to 200 pounds are also caught in the lagoon. Candlefish are taken with dip nets. Runs of American shad occur from May through July.

The Klamath Beach Road runs up the estuary, passing beneath the US 101 bridge before it enters the Coast Indian Community

Reservation. This is a small settlement. The 87,500-acre Hoopa Valley Indian Reservation begins twenty miles upriver. It's one of four large reservations in California created by Congress in 1864. The bulk of the land lies on the Trinity River, but frontage on both sides of the Klamath River was added by President Harrison in 1891. The present population is estimated at 5,000 Hupas and Yuroks with small representation from perhaps a dozen other tribes.

By the standards of the small rancherias, the Indians of the Hoopa Valley Reservation are relatively prosperous. Some obtain an income from timber receipts. Some are college-educated and operate resorts, saw mills, and other businesses. Yet employment opportunities are limited and more than a few families live in poverty with little or no aid from public agencies.

Several times, the Yuroks were forced to withdraw from the river by the early settlers but they never accepted defeat. They wage war now in the arena of the courts. Often, they find themselves at odds with the Bureau of Indian Affairs.

A sample grievance is illustrated by the $987,000 appropriated by Congress for repair of Indian homes in Northern California damaged by the 1964 flood. About $270,000 of this amount was diverted by the Bureau of Indian Affairs to other states. Of the funds that were left, much was wasted. All-electric homes of shabby construction were installed on the Klamath River at locations twenty miles from the nearest power line.

An exit off the Klamath Beach Road leads to the US 101 Highway.

Statues of golden bears guard the portals of the Highway 101 bridge as they did on the old span which was washed out by the 1964 flood. The deluge destroyed several resorts and the village of Klamath.

Just across the bridge is the exit to the Starwein Road. This

97

*The Alder Camp Road approaches the Klamath
River from Prairie Creek State Park.*

road runs four miles upriver to Klamath Glen. The village sprawls on a flat below the Terwar Valley where Fort Terwar was garrisoned in 1855 to oversee the Indians. After the fort was damaged by a flood in 1862, the soldiers moved to a post on the Smith River.

The Starwein Road peters out at Starwein Flat, 1½ miles upriver from Klamath Glen. For thirteen miles, no road follows either bank of the Klamath. A highway is planned but there is much local opposition to it, especially among the Indians. Timm Williams, a Yurok leader, claims it would disturb the ecology and run through Indian villages and burial grounds.

Between the 101 bridge and Starwein Flat are MacDonald, Waukel, Turwar, Glen, Blake, and Tarup Riffles, all productive of steelhead trout when the runs begin in late August. Many good riffles may be approached by boat on the roadless stretch of the river. Fishermen in boot foot waders work the riffles with spoons, spinners, small plugs, bait, and wet streamer flies. Among the proven patterns are the Royal Coachman, Thor, Mickey Finn, Umpqua, and Green Drake.

Autumn fly fishing calls for the same tackle as used for winter steelhead with a weight-forward "shooting head" fly line. For lure and bait casting, a seven-foot spinning rod of light to medium weight is favored.

A light salt water casting outfit is right for salmon. However, boat fishermen prefer a 6-8′ boat rod and star drag reel spooled with 30 to 40 pound test line.

The early runs of steelhead are largely composed of "half-pounders," which is the local name for sea trout in the one- to three-pound weight range. These are very sporty fish which invariably break water when hooked. As the season wears on, the steelhead tend to run larger. After December rains roil and raise the river, the best fishing is found upstream off State Highway 96. Felt soles are recommended for wading the riffles because the stream bottom is very slippery.

A 10 H.P. motor will suffice for trips upriver. But 25 H.P. is not too much if you plan to fish anywhere near the entrance to the lagoon.

Returning to US 101, there are a number of turn-offs within a mile or so of the bridge. One leads to Camp Klamath and one to the Simpson Timber Company where visitors are welcome to tour the plant. Just off the highway is the depot of the Klamath & Hoppaw Valley Railroad. The line operates a summer excursion train on four miles of track salvaged from a logging operation.

On the same side of the road is the new Klamath townsite which replaces the village destroyed by the 1964 flood. It was developed with federal aid at a cost of $5 million. The post office, jail, and courthouse were dedicated in 1969. The site is dyked by the highway and is four feet higher than the river has ever been known to rise.

Two miles from the bridge is the exit for Requa. A short drive brings us to a forks of the road at the picturesque old Requa Inn.

The mouth of the Klamath Road winds down to a resort area on the lagoon where there's boat launching and fee access to shore fishing.

The Patrick Murphy Memorial Drive climbs to an Air Force radar base on the steep headland which abuts the north bank of the lagoon. Off this road about ½-mile from the inn, a dim unsigned lane approaches a redwood dwelling known as "Lye-eck." This is an old family home of the Yurok which has been restored by the Del Norte Historical Society.

The rough boards and planks were hewn with an adze of elk horn driven by a stone hammer. There were 24 family homes

100

and thirteen sweathouses before Requa was raided in the 1870's by some Tolowa Indians from Crescent City. The Tolowas attacked because they believed a shaman at Requa had worked magic to stop salmon from entering the Smith River.

"Lye-eck" overlooks the lagoon with a clear view of the rock Oregos.

Homage is paid to Oregos and the other spirits at the Salmon Festival which is held at Klamath townsite in late June just before the resorts become filled. The Festival is a blend of country fair, Indian culture, and Chamber of Commerce hokum. Mostly the attendance is local with a big turn-out from Crescent City. Everybody on the river comes—loggers, ranchers, mill workers, townspeople, and soldiers from the Air Base. The older Indians come dressed in conventional street clothes; the teenagers in their blue jeans or hippie garb are hard to pick out among the Caucasian youths with whom they attend the same schools.

There are pony rides, bingo games, "games of skill," art-in-action, and booths which sell cakes, pies, paintings, and Indian beadwork. There are displays of fine Yurok baskets which can't be had for any price.

After the notables make their speeches, the Princess of the Salmon Festival is crowned. This will be an Indian maiden selected from several contestants dressed in ancient finery. Then the sacred songs and dances begin. The first dance is not genuine because the men wear bonnets of turkey feathers. A spokesman for the group explains this is done to convince skeptics who might question whether they are true American Indians. But then the bonnets are exchanged for authentic red head bands that are decorated with the scalps of woodpeckers.

There follows the Brush Dance, the World Renewal Dance, and perhaps the Dance of the White Deer Skin. Only the men dance but at times the women sing.

Afterwards, there are performances by rock and roll bands, some of which are Indian.

A salmon barbeque is held on tables spread out in a meadow. Then the crowd divides to watch boat races, motorcycle acrobatics, and logging contests. The largest audience gathers for the rough and tumble Indian stick game played between a local team and Indians from Crescent City.

For centuries, the spirit of Oregos has prevailed over all adversity but the day may come when the salmon runs up the Klamath are halted forever. This will surely happen if the State Water Plan is carried to completion.

Presently, the Plan calls for a chain of high dams which would impound the major tributaries of the Klamath and the main river down to the mouth. However, opposition to the project is growing and conservation groups have only begun to mount a campaign against it. Recently, seven California Congressmen co-sponsored a bill which would have the Eel, Trinity, and Klamath Rivers included in the national wild and scenic rivers systems. If the legislation was approved, it would effectively block further dam building on these rivers.

Wilson Creek Beach is a popular spot to net surf smelt.

A large fishing fleet is based at Crescent Harbor.

CHAPTER 23: CRESCENT CITY AND THE SMITH RIVER   On his trail-blazing expedition up the Redwood Coast, the mountain man, Jedediah Smith, camped near the present site of Crescent City and logged the low coastal plain in his journal.

Smith's discoveries on this journey of 1828 were largely ignored by the outside world. The only interest was on the part of fur trappers anxious to find an overland route to California from the Pacific Northwest.

Settlement, when it came to Crescent Bay in the 1850's, was sparked by a colorful legend.

There were many versions of the legend but, in substance, it told of a solitary prospector who trekked over the Coast Range and found a rich vein of gold near the seashore. The miner built a cabin and worked the strike for quite some time, taking care to hide the treasure he accumulated in a cleverly concealed place. Then, one day, he was attacked by Indians who burned the cabin and left him for dead.

Half out of his mind, the gravely injured man somehow managed to make his way back to civilization. Here he told a few close friends where his gold was buried just before he died of his wounds.

The tale as it was circulated in the Forty-Niner camps apparently contained some details which pointed to the Smith River area as the probable location. It was on a search for the "lost cabin" that a party of prospectors sighted Crescent Bay in the Spring of 1851. This discovery was investigated by a party that came down from Althouse, Oregon. The group decided the bay had possibilities as a port and dispatched a delegate to San Francisco to find a backer. In the fall of 1852, the schooner, Pomona, arrived with supplies and a band of settlers headed by J. H. Wendell.

Largest island off Pebble Beach is brooding Castle Rock.

The townsite for Crescent City was laid out in February 1853. Within a year, 300 buildings had been erected.

For some years, Crescent City flourished as a shipping point for the diggings in southwest Oregon. It also vied with Trinidad and the ports on Humboldt Bay for the trade of the Klamath mines. Optimism for the town's future knew no bounds when it took over the county seat from Trinidad in 1854.

The price of city lots was driven out of sight by speculators. A furious campaign was launched to make Crescent City the capital of California. Families from the East were lured to emigrate here on the promise the town would soon overtake San Francisco.

The bubble burst in 1855 when the county seat was shifted to Orleans Bar. But there was fresh excitement the following year when gold was discovered only six miles outside the city limits.

The last big strikes in the Smith River watershed were made in the 1870's. By then, lumbering was nearly established as the dominant enterprise of Crescent City.

On the drive to Crescent City from the Klamath River, we dip low to a patch of sandy seashore and then wheel through the virgin forest of the 6,375-acre Del Norte Redwoods State Park.

From the bridge, it's three miles to a resort known as "Trees of Mystery." The main interest here is some deformed redwoods.

A mile farther, we arrive on the coast at False Klamath Cove. Here is twelve-acre Lagoon Creek County Park, a new preserve, developed with state and federal aid. The lagoon is an old millpond filled with water lilies and rainbow trout. There's a small picnic area with benches, tables, stoves, and restrooms. The beach abounds with driftwood. Two trails leave the park.

The Yurok Loop Trail runs ten miles. It's a 2½-mile hike to the Klamath River Overlook by way of the Coastal Trail.

The park abuts the Wilson Creek Beach located just inside

It's a 200-yard walk to the Battery Point
Lighthouse at low tide.

the south boundary of the Del Norte Redwoods. Jedediah Smith's party feasted on elk steaks here. It's a popular spot to net surf smelt. Salmon, steelhead, and a few cutthroat enter the creek after winter rains open the bar.

From Wilson Creek, the road veers inland and climbs to an elevation 1,200 feet above the sea on its nine-mile run through the redwoods.

Three miles beyond Wilson Creek is the Henry Solon Memorial Grove. From here, the Damnation Creek Trail winds 2½ miles through giant ferns and lush shrubbery in a semi-rain forest. The steep hike ends at a rocky beach where there are tide pools.

Near the north boundary of the park, a side road snakes down to park headquarters and a new 142-site campground on a fork of Mill Creek. The area is located outside the fog belt in second-growth redwoods. About 100 sites will accommodate trailers. The washrooms have hot showers and laundry facilities. There's summer trout fishing on Mill Creek and sixteen miles of trails.

Park wildlife includes ruffed grouse, foxes, wildcats, bears, and blacktail deer. Roosevelt elk are occasionally seen.

Shortly after we leave the park, the forest opens to expose the long graceful sweep of Crescent Beach. Driftwood is abundant here. In the fever of the Gold Rush, every square foot of this beach was staked out with mining claims.

Crescent Harbor lies at the west end of the beach. It's protected by rock jetties that are reinforced with hundreds of tetrapods. A French invention which resemble playing jacks, the tetrapods weigh 25 tons each. One stands as a memorial where US 101 crosses the city limits.

On the east side of the harbor is the Citizen's Dock, a public wharf built entirely with private donations of money, equipment, and materials. Crescent City has always been strong on community effort. When mining petered out in the 1870's, the lead-

US Highway 199 follows the Smith River through the redwoods of Jedediah Smith State Park.

ing citizens organized a cooperative saw mill. It was built on Lake Earl and operated successfully until destroyed by fire in the 1890's.

Sportsmen come to the Citizen's Dock to launch their boats; youngsters gather here when school is out to fish for perch and jack smelt.

A light spinning outfit works well for pier fishing. But all a small child needs to catch perch is some bait and a simple hand line with a clamp-on sinker and a No. 8 hook. No California angling license is required for salt water fishing off a public pier.

A number of fish buyers have stations on the dock where visitors may watch the commercial boats unload shrimp, crabs, rockfish, and salmon. The activity is brisk most evenings in Summer, but here as elsewhere on the North Coast the fishing industry has its share of woes.

A live issue is the competition from the modern fleets of Japan and the Soviet Union which fish North Coast waters just outside the 12 mile limit. There's concern about the threat of ocean pollution.

From the Citizen's Dock, it's one mile to city limits.

Crescent City lies near the south end of the Smith River plain which is eight miles deep and 25 miles long. About two-thirds of Del Norte County's 19,000 population lives here. Next to lumbering, the important industries are recreation, dairy farming, commercial fishing, and the growing of Easter lily bulbs. A small enterprise is the packaging of decorative greenery, such as ferns, huckleberry and redwood boughs for Eastern markets.

The plain is cool and foggy, with a summer temperature that averages 61 degrees. A warmer, sunnier summer climate is found just a few miles inland where the mountains begin.

With its new shops and park-like waterfront, Crescent City has a contemporary look which belies its romantic past. This

111

Fog and driftwood abound at Pelican State Beach.

largely results from the monstrous tidal wave which destroyed the old business district on March 28, 1964.

Among the few remnants of the early days is the Battery Point Lighthouse which is perched on a rocky isle off the foot of Battery Street. Built in 1856, the light station serves as a museum. It's a 200 yard walk from the beach at low tide.

The museum of the Del Norte Historical Society at 640 "H" Street contains Indian artifacts and relics of the pioneer settlement. Antiques fill the McNulty Museum, located a block away at Fifth and "H" Streets.

Pebble Beach stretches north from Battery Point to Point St. George. It's fronted by a scenic drive from which numerous trails and stairways approach the shore. The beach is popular with fishermen and driftwood collectors; rockhounds find agates, jade, and petrified wood on it. The charm of this beach is enhanced by a number of rocky islets with pines growing on them.

At the intersection of the drive with Ninth Street, an historical marker memorializes the loss of the Brother Jonathan. On a stormy day in the summer of 1865, this coastwise steamer foundered on the rocks as it was attempting to enter the harbor. Of 232 passengers and crew, only nineteen persons survived.

The St. George Light, located seven miles off the coast, has provided a beacon for mariners since 1891. The rock tower, which is 146 feet tall, required four years to build.

The Pebble Beach Drive terminates at Point St. George where there's good rock fishing and skin diving. A small county park affords access to the miles of lonely beach which extend north of the point to the mouth of the Smith River. Here there's perch fishing, smelt netting, and beds of little neck, Washington, and razor clams.

Four miles northeast of town, the Redwood Highway forks. US 101 swings north to approach the Smith River estuary. US

*Picnic area in the Jedediah Smith Redwoods
adjoins a swimming beach on the Smith River.*

Highway 199 bears east to enter the redwoods of Jedediah Smith State Park.

If you're not towing a trailer, the more interesting approach to the Jedediah Smith Redwoods is by way of the Howland Hill Road. This is a remnant of the old stage road which ran to Sailor Diggings and other mining camps in southwest Oregon. It was known as the "Crescent City and Yreka Plank Turnpike Road" when it was built in 1858.

On this drive, we leave US 101 southeast of town on the Elk Valley Road. It's about a mile to the junction with the Howland Hill Road at the Crescent City Indian Reservation.

Another mile brings us to the steep grade which crests on Howland Summit. It was here Crescent City's first lumber mill, built by F. E. Weston in 1853, obtained timber. The logs were hauled to town on a wagon with wheels twelve feet in diameter.

From Howland Summit, the narrow, unpaved road inclines gently through the heart of the Jedediah Smith Redwoods. The road joins Highway 199 just outside the northeast corner of the park in the Six Rivers National Forest.

Proceeding west on US 199, it's a short run to the developed area of the park. There's a large campground where raccoons raid food left out at night and an attractive swimming beach on the Smith River. A number of trails leave the area for nature walks. One approaches the Stout Grove said to contain the heaviest stand of timber on the coast. The largest redwood measures twenty feet in diameter and 340 feet tall.

On a stroll along the banks of the Smith, you may see otters playing in the riffles. Summer fishing is good for rainbow and cutthroat trout. In winter, there's steelhead fishing on the main river and the Middle Fork upstream to Patrick Creek in the National Forest.

The Smith River estuary may be approached on the North

Damnation Creek trail winds through semi-rain forest to an isolated spot on the seashore of Del Norte Redwoods State Park.

Bank Road, an eight-mile scenic drive which leaves US 199 near park headquarters.

The plain north of Crescent City may be explored on the Lake Earl Drive. This by-passed section of Old US 101 forks off the Redwood Highway just north of city limits. From the junction, it's six miles to the Lake Earl Road which affords access to a small boat launching site on Lake Earl.

The lake is a 2,000-acre freshwater lagoon, fringed with tules and remnants of a great forest that was destroyed by early logging. A slender neck of water connects the lake with a small seaside lagoon known as Lake Talawa. Salmon, steelhead, sturgeon, and other fish enter Lake Talawa when it spills over to the sea during winters of heavy rainfall.

Trolling for cutthroat trout at Lake Earl is best in late autumn and winter. There's duck hunting on the lagoon in season.

The Lake Earl Drive runs north through dreary cut-over land to Fort Dick which has a cheese plant. The hamlet was named for a nearby farm, known as Dick's Fort, where the settlers took refuge from the Indians. A trifle north of Fort Dick, the road joins US 101 just before it crosses the Smith River on the Dr. Fine Bridge.

On the north bank, the Fred Haight Drive leaves the highway to approach the Smith River Angling Access where there's boat launching.

It's three miles to the village of Smith River on Rowdy Creek. This is a dairy and lumbering center where the Easter Lily Festival is held in July. Most of the potted Easter lilies sold in this country come from bulbs grown in the Crescent City area and just across the state line at Harbor, Oregon. The industry got started here after imports of bulbs from Japan ceased in World War II.

We pass the large bulb farm of Dahlstrom and Watt on the Sarina Road which leaves the Redwood Highway 1½ miles

*Virgin forest lines the banks of the Smith River
in the Jedediah Smith Redwoods State Park.*

118

west of Smith River. The lilies bloom in the fields here during July. Bulbs which produce flowers in time for Easter are "forced" by florists in hot houses.

Lily bulbs are a high risk crop which call for an investment of as much as $10,000 an acre. Two growing seasons are required before the bulbs may be harvested. The most popular strains are the Ace and Nellie White, which are varieties of Erabus.

The Sarina Road terminates at a large fishing resort situated where Rowdy Creek enters the Smith River.

Returning to US 101, it's two miles farther to the fishing resorts clustered near the rivermouth in the vicinity of Salmon Harbor. Here is a duplication of the facilities found on the Klamath River lagoon. A landmark is the Ship Ashore Restaurant. It's housed in the S.S. Castle Rock, a 480-ton steel ship which was used by the Navy in World War II.

The Smith is only a shade less renowned than the Klamath as an angling river. Each year, it yields trophy steelhead to 20 pounds and king salmon to 50 pounds. The best fishing gets underway just when the action on the lower Klamath begins to slow.

October is the peak month for king salmon. This is when skiff fishermen anchor gunwale-to-gunwale across the lower estuary in rows known as "hog lines."

The fall migration of silver salmon arrives in November.

The early run of steelhead known as "half-pounders" peaks in late October. The trophy fish show in December and January.

The Smith supports the best fishing for sea-run cutthroat trout in California. Spring and Autumn afford the peak action. The services of a professional guide are recommended because the productive water is highly localized. The east end of Tillas Island is apt to be rewarding in May. Spoons, wet flies, and strip bait trolled on a No. 2 hook are the favorite offerings.

119

The Mouth of the Smith River Road affords access to Pyramid Point where there's good casting for perch and flounder.

Where US 101 turns away from the mouth, it passes through the Smith River Indian Reservation. Just up the road is Clifford Kamph Memorial Park, a county preserve with beach access and picnic benches.

The last stop is Pelican State Beach. This undeveloped frontage is usually fog-bound and deserted but it holds a treasure trove of driftwood.

BIBLIOGRAPHY

Adams, Kramer. *The Redwoods*. New York: Popular Library.

Aginsky, B. W. and E. G. *Deep Valley*. New York: Stein and Day, 1967.

Andrews, Ralph W. *Redwood Classic*. Seattle: Superior Publishing Company, 1958.

Bowers, Nathan A. *Cone Bearing Trees of the Pacific Coast*. Palo Alto, California: Pacific Books, 1942.

Braun, Ernest, and Brown, Vinson. *Exploring Pacific Coast Tidepools*. Healdsburg, California: Naturegraph Publishing, 1966.

Bronson, William. *How to Kill a Golden State*. Garden City, New York: Doubleday & Company, Inc., 1968.

Chase, J. Smeaton. *California Coast Trails*. Boston and New York: Houghton Mifflin Co., 1913.

Crump, Spencer. *The Story of the Western Skunk Railroad*. Los Angeles: Trans-Anglo Books, 1963.

Dasmann, William P. *Big Game of California*. Sacramento, California: California Department of Fish and Game, 1958.

Davis, William Morris. *The Lakes of California,* California Journal of Mines and Geology, Vol. 44, No. 2. San Francisco: Division of Mines, April 1948.

Dickinson, A. Bray. *Narrow Gauge to the Redwoods*. Los Angeles: Trans-Anglo Books, 1967.

Ellison, William Henry. *A Self Governing Dominion, California 1849-1860*. Berkeley and Los Angeles: University of California Press, 1950.

Fitch, John E. *Offshore Fishes of California*. Sacramento, California: California Department of Fish and Game, 1958.

Gibbs, James A. *Shipwrecks of the Pacific Coast*. Portland, Oregon: Binfords & Mort, 1957.

Gudde, Erwin G. *California Place Names*. Berkeley and Los Angeles: University of California Press, 1965.

Hansen and Miller. *Wild Oats in Eden*. Santa Rosa, California: 1962.

Hinds, Norman E. *Evolution of the California Landscape,* Bulletin 158. San Francisco: California Division of Mines, 1952.

Hoopes, Chad L. *Lure of Humboldt Bay Region*. 135 South Locust Street, Dubuque, Iowa: William C. Brown Co., 1966.

121

Hoover and Rensch. *Historic Spots in California.* Stanford, California: Stanford University Press.

Hyde, Phillip, and Leydet, Francois. *The Last Redwoods.* San Francisco: The Sierra Club, 1963.

Ingles, Lloyd Glenn. *Mammals of California and Its Coastal Waters.* Stanford, California: Stanford University Press, 1957.

Jepsen, Willis L. *Trees, Shrubs, and Flowers of the Redwood Region.* Save-the-Redwoods League.

Kirker, Harold. *California's Architectural Frontier.* San Marino, California: The Huntington Library, 1960.

Kneiss, Gilbert H. *Redwood Railways.* Berkeley, California: Howell-North, 1956.

Kroeber, A. L. *Handbook of the Indians of California.* Washington, D. C.: Smithsonian Institute, Bulletin 78, 1925.

Lantis, Steiner, and Karinen. *California: Land of Contrast.* Belmont, California: Wadsworth Publishing Co., 1963.

McNairn, Jack, and MacMullen, Jerry. *Ships of the Redwood Coast.* Stanford, California: Stanford University Press, 1945.

Miller, Jeanne Thurlow. *Seeing Historic Sonoma County Today.* Santa Rosa, California: The Miller Associates, 1967.

Moungovan and Escola. *Where There's a Will, There's a Way; Unusual Logging and Lumbering Methods on the Mendocino Coast.* Mendocino County Historical Society, 1968.

Munz, Philip A. *California Spring Wildflowers.* Berkeley and Los Angeles: University of California Press, 1961.

Newell, Gordon, and Williamson, Joe. *Pacific Lumber Ships.* Seattle, Washington: Superior Publishing Co., 1960.

Nixon, Stuart, *Redwood Empire.* New York: E. P. Dutton & Co., Inc., 1966.

Phillips, Julius B. *A Review of the Rockfishes of California,* Fish Bulletin 104. California Department of Fish and Game, Marine Fisheries Branch, 1957.

————. *The Commercial Fish Catch of California for the Year 1947 with an Historical Review, 1916-1947.* State of California, Division of Fish and Game, Fish Bulletin No. 74, 1949.

122

Powers, Alfred. *Redwood Country*. New York: Duell, Sloan & Pearce, 1949.

Praag, Greta Van. *How They Won the War for Bolinas Lagoon*. San Francisco: San Francisco magazine: 1970.

Robinson, John. *The Redwood Highway*. California Highways and Public Works, May-June 1964, September-October 1964.

Roedel, Phil M. *Common Ocean Fishes of the California Coast,* Fish Bulletin 91. California Department of Fish and Game, 1953.

Rowntree, Lester. *Flowering Shrubs of California*. Stanford, California: Stanford University Press, second edition, 1948.

Smith, Esther Ruth. *The History of Del Norte County*. Oakland, California: The Holmes Book Co., 1953.

Thompson, R. A. *Fort Ross*. Oakland, California: Bio-books, 1951.

Wales, J. H. *Trout of California*. Sacramento, California: California Department of Fish and Game: 1957.

———. *Waterfowl of California*. Sacramento, California: California Department of Fish and Game: 1956.

Warburton and Endert. *Indian Lore of the Northern California Coast*. Santa Clara, California: Pacific Pueblo Press, 1966.

———. *Drakes Plate of Brass*. San Francisco: California Historical Society, 1937.

———. *The Russians in California*. San Francisco: California Historical Society, 1933.

———. *California's Historical Landmarks*. State of California Resources Agency, Division of Beaches and Parks.

Progress Report to the Governor and Legislature by State Advisory Commission on Indian Affairs. Senate Bill No. 1007 on Indians in Rural and Reservation Areas, 1966.

———. *North Coast Tour Booklet*. Fort Bragg, California: Mendocino County Historical Society, 1959.

———. *The California Coast Redwood*. U. S. Department of Agriculture, Forest Service, October 1964.

———. *California Western Railroad*. San Mateo, California: Super Skunk Edition, The Western Railroader, August 1965.

123

NEWSPAPERS:

San Francisco Chronicle
San Francisco Examiner
Oakland-Tribune
Mendocino Beacon
Humboldt Times-Standard
Sacramento Bee
Fort Bragg Advocate-News
Del Norte Triplicate and American

MAPS:

Ocean Fishing Map of Del Norte, Humboldt, and Mendocino Counties (12-64)

Ocean Fishing Map of Sonoma and Marin Counties (8-64)

Angler's Guide to the Klamath River (11-67)

Salmon and Steelhead Fishing Map (11-60)
State of California, Department of Fish and Game, Sacramento, Calif.

INFORMATION SOURCES:

Bureau of Land Management, 168 Washington Street, Ukiah, California 95482

Del Norte Chamber of Commerce, P. O. Box 698, Crescent City, California 95531

Greater Eureka Chamber of Commerce, 2112 Broadway, Eureka, California

Department of Fish and Game, Regional Offices: Ferry Building, San Francisco, and 619 Second Street, Eureka, California

Jackson State Forest, Fort Bragg, California

Mendocino County Information, P. O. Box 244, Ukiah, California

Redwood Empire Association, 476 Post Street, San Francisco, California 94102

Department of Parks and Recreation, P. O. Box 2390, Sacramento, California 95811

Marin Visitors Bureau, 801 "B" Street, San Rafael, California

Russian River Region, Inc., Box 255, Guerneville, California

Redwood National Park—Visitors Information Offices are located at Orick and Crescent City, California

124

INDEX

126